SHREE SAI BABA

OF

SOUTH SAN FRANCISCO

DEVOTEES SPEAK

SHREE SAI BABA

OF

SOUTH SAN FRANCISCO

DEVOTEES SPEAK

GWYN MCGEE

Beyond Maya Press

BEYOND MAYA PRESS

SHREE SAI BABA of South San Francisco: DEVOTEES SPEAK

Cover Design: Steve L. Patterson

Cover Photo Mosaic: Shekhar Surabhi

Cover Photo: Gwyn F. McGee

ISBN: 978-0-9834270-3-2

Copyright © 2013 Gwyn F. McGee

DEDICATION

Most Loving Of All,
May we recognize Your Precious Feet in All Forms

You are surprised that I can be in two bodies at the same time,
or in a thousand different places.
~Sathya Sai Baba~

- Sathyam Sivam Sundaram Part 4, Page 194

QUOTES FROM SAI BABA OF SHIRDI'S GYARAH VACHAN

~I shall be ever active and vigorous even after leaving this earthly body.~

~My mortal remains would speak from the tomb.~

EXCERPTS FROM SATHYA SAI BABA'S DIVINE DISCOURSE, PRASHANTI NILIYAM, JANUARY 14, 1999

"As Narsimhamurthi pointed out Kasturi once urged Me not to neglect this body in the process of saving a devotee. I replied that this body has come for the sake of devotees and shall be utilized for doing anything and everything for their welfare. Body attachment is human and total detachment is divine. Attachment to the body is responsible for all suffering and misery. Since God does not have any body attachment, He does not attach any importance to the suffering of His body. Once He assumes a body, many things are bound to happen to the body. Whatever happens is for the welfare of the whole world."

"Likewise, I take upon Myself the untold suffering of students and devotees at various points of time in order to protect them."

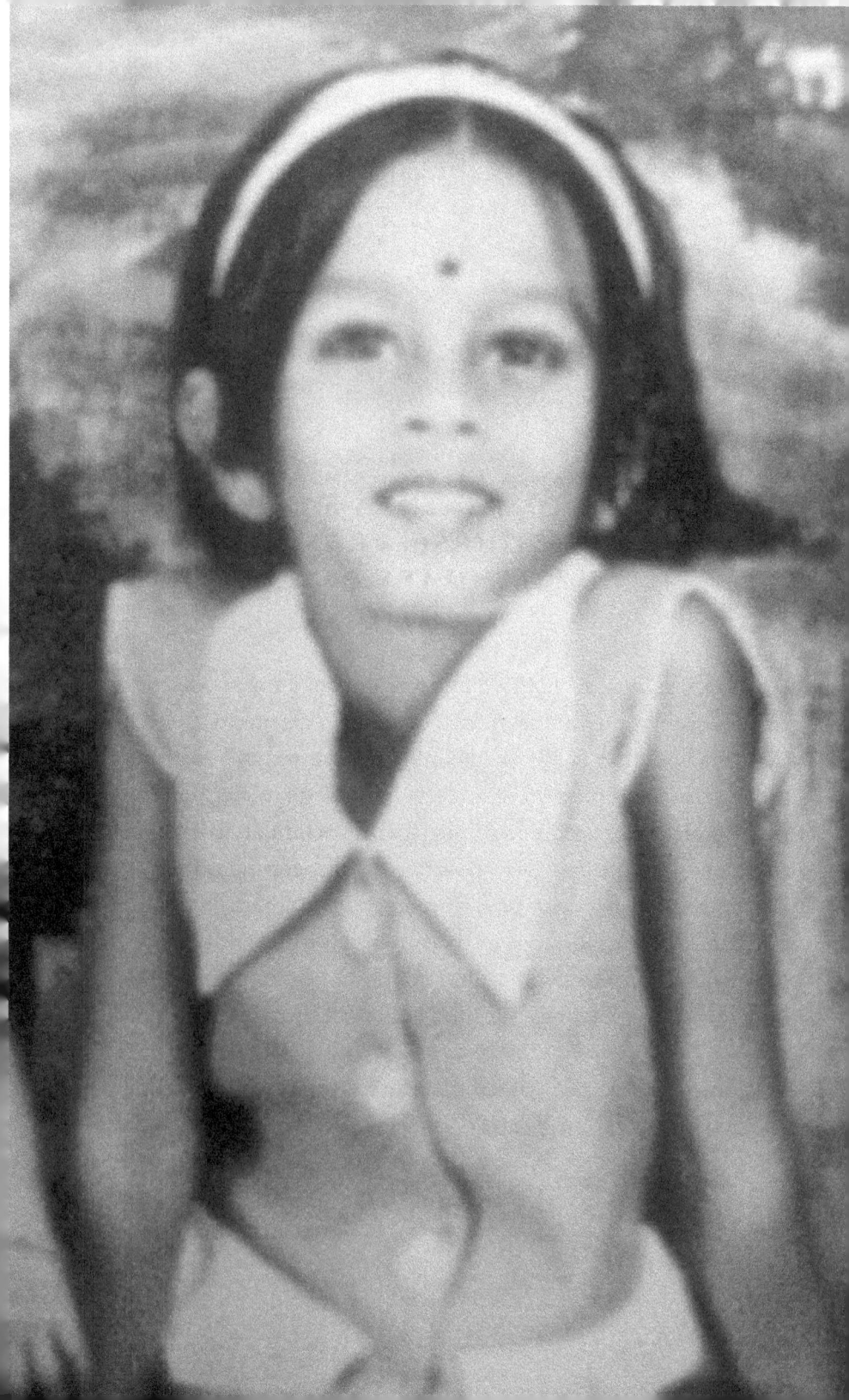

SHREE LAL

"I don't know how long I'm going to be here...if this is the place for me. Taking people's pain is a lot for me."

Miracles occurred when I was a child but I wasn't aware of what was actually happening. The point in my life when I absolutely knew something extraordinary was taking place was when Baba started coming in 1997.

My mom (Parvati Lal) took me to India that year; to Kodaikanal because I had a brain tumor. I had been paralyzed for two months and was taking chemotherapy at Stanford University. I didn't really know who Sathya Sai Baba was; my mom was a Sathya Sai devotee; I was into Shirdi Baba.

We were there when Sathya Sai Baba gave darshan at His ashram one day and I began to speak to Him inside myself. "If you're God, you are going to call me for interview and you are going to heal me."

I was called for an interview and all I could do was cry. Suddenly, I didn't see Sathya Sai Baba in that physical form; I saw Shirdi Baba. Yet... I still had my doubts. So I thought, if He is really God He is going to put His hands on my head and He's going to talk to me. The moment I said that to myself this man approached me.

"Are you from the US?" he asked.

"Yes."

"Baba wants to see you."

I went in to see Baba and I was crying and crying and crying and crying.

"Why fear when I am here?" Baba said to me.

Oh my God, I thought, and I stop crying.

"Tumor?" He placed His hand on my head. "No tumor."

After that Baba looked at my hand and commented on the four sections of my fingers.

"We are connected," He proclaimed.

I started to cry again and all I could ask for was vibhuti.

We returned to the states and I went back to Stanford University. It was a miracle. I had no tumor. Nothing. After that... everything started.

In the beginning when 'Baba came' I spoke what He called a universal language. No one understood it but Him. Baba would come to me and I became a form of someone I could not see. People around me received Baba's darshan and they would say Baba came and He did this and He did that and....

"Who am I?" I would cry frustrated. "I know I am some kind of form that is talking but I'm a jyoti...a tiny flame; I can't see myself. I can't!" and my frustration mounted. "Why can't I receive Baba's darshan? This is unfair."

So I told Baba. "I want to see You. I want to see the Form. I want to see Who I Am. I want to see this Form in me."

After that Baba started visiting me at two o'clock...three o'clock in the morning. He talked to me about a lot of things. Many things I cannot say. He talked to me about me.

2

"You're on Earth now," Baba said and He explained what was happening to me...what would be my life. Once Baba told me who I was when I was in Shirdi after a devotee accidentally told me what Baba shared during a darshan. I didn't want to believe what they told me and I could not sleep that night. So I asked Baba.

He said, "You were the little girl Jeepree. You had leprosy and I healed you."

After Baba told me that I cried. "I can't be that. If I was that I was untouchable and no one could touch me and everyone was against me."

"I know you're upset," Baba comforted me. "But look at where you are today. Everyone wants to touch you."

Sometimes, because I take people's pain, I cry and ask, "Why?" But then Baba comes and explains...and I say, "Okay. I am the chosen one."

So if someone today asked me why I am always sick? Why do you take everyone's pain? This is what I would say:

Years ago I asked God...Baba, "What can I do to be close to you in this life? I don't want attachments."

He said, "But you're on Earth. You already have attachments."

"I want to be attached to You," I replied. "I want to be close to You. What do I do?"

"But if you are attached to Me...if you are close to Me...you will have too much pain."

That's when I said, "If I can have the whole world's pain to be the closest one to You...to be one-on-one with You, I will take all the pain." That is why I am the chosen one. I asked for it.

After I asked I noticed I became sicker and sicker and sicker. When I am in the depths of sickness He comes and explains this is what you asked for. I truly can not complain; but some

---

days I say, "Why, Baba? Why?" Yet deep down inside I know the answer. I asked for it. I wanted to be close to God.

Baba warned me, "If you want to be very close to Me. If you want to be one-on-one, then that's pain."

But Baba also promised something He has done. "I will lift you up," He told me. "I will uplift you to be able to take the pain that is given."

That is why when I go to the hospitals they poke me everywhere but yet they don't find anything ... because there is nothing wrong with this body. It is the people's pain.

I have adapted to the fact that I am close to God and there is nothing beyond that. I have accepted if taking the pain of the world allows me to be close to God...then that's what I'll do. God takes on the suffering of the world so there will be less of it. That is God. God is within everyone, but there are certain people who can take on this kind of task. Baba has told me there will come a time when my suffering ends. He did not tell me when, but that is why I keep doing certain things that others may not understand I have to do. And for those who do not believe what is occurring here...I cannot make them believe. It is not time for them to believe. When the time is right...they will believe. But I don't have to prove myself to others... prove what goes through this body. I know Who I Am connected with and that is all that matters. Just like in Shirdi, there were only certain devotees who were the true, true devotees of Baba. People come to Shirdi; people pray to Shirdi and people go. It is the same with me. People will come and they will see Baba; they will have experiences and they will move on. Some people stay. They know.

Note:

As I ended the interview with Shree sitting perhaps a foot and half from her on a couch, the most wonderful, unexpected scent billowed around us.

"Do you smell that? That perfume?" I asked. "Is that coming off of you?"

I leaned toward her and I knew the answer. "It is coming from you," I said, keenly aware of how the divine scent punctuated and validated all that was shared.

Her smile and voice were sweet when she replied, "Kind of. A little bit, no? These kinds of things happen to me, sometimes."

Baba's Chair

"BABA HAS COME"

MRIDU ARYA

When I made my first visit to the South San Francisco mandir in 2010 I was pretty skeptical. You hear about impostors posing as gurus and I gave it a try because Bharat (Kona) bhaiya insisted so much. I was looking for some help so I thought what if I could find my answers here. Until I met Baba I was looking for a guru who could lead me. So during my first visit I think my skepticism stopped me from feeling anything. I tried to meditate and feel the energy around me but I didn't feel anything. Baba came and I went up to Him. I asked a very simple question, "What career do you think I should pick in my life?"

"Management," He replied.

I went back to my seat and that was the end of it. My first visit was very ordinary.

Bharat bhaiya insisted that I ask more questions of Baba so I went back. I was too shy to ask some of my personal questions because Bakul (Patel) and Ashu (Asish Chandra) bhaiya were there. I didn't want to talk about my love life in front of them. After that trip I thought this is the last time I am going to do this, no matter what Bharat bhaiya says. I am done with this place.

After bhajans that day the majority of the people had gone home and there were just a few of us left with Shree. I left the room and came back again to tell Bharat bhaiya, Let's go. All of a sudden Oreo, the dog in the house, started barking at me and wouldn't stop. At that point Shree started looking at me. Finally they took Oreo out of the room because of his barking. That's when Shree began to ask me questions. "What is your name? You are a very nice person. How old are you? Have you gone through a heart-break? Did you get disappointed a lot of times in your relationship?"

After she asked those last questions I thought, how is it that she knows all of this?

I started to pay more attention to what she was saying. Shree started telling me things about my past, not only things about my past that happened but she began to answer questions. These were questions that I had in my mind for so many years. She began to give me answers that made so much sense. Questions I had asked my friends at a time when things seemed twisted and confusing. Shree told me the answers with so much clarity literally my jaw dropped. She told me all these things during my second visit; the visit when I had determined I would not come back. I am so grateful to Baba that He told Shree to tell me all these things.

During that time I was grieving over my ex. Shree told me why our relationship failed. She told me the answers behind the questions and she told me when the proper time came I would move on.

A year passed and I was still very shy about asking Baba questions. Bharat bhaiya was the one who continued to ask questions for me. My ex became engaged and Baba told us

He did not reveal what was happening with my ex because He knew it would cause me a lot of pain. My faith in Baba increased so much after that because when I found out my ex was engaged I could not sleep for two weeks. I might sleep for half an hour, not quite an hour, and then I would wake up in a lot of emotional pain. During that time Shree became pregnant with Shivam and Baba stop coming. Although Baba was not coming to Shree he came to me in a dream. He came in a form that was so big it was frightening. When I said, "What is this?" He shrank to a size smaller than me. Baba placed His hand on my head and I felt this tingling sensation as it rested there. I was in so much emotional pain that I couldn't speak, and Baba said, "Bolo Beta." There was so much love in His voice when He said it. I choked up and I couldn't speak. I was very close to my father and he was the only one who called me Beta.

All of a sudden I felt such peace. Then I thought, "Wait a minute. Is this a dream?" If it's reality I want to see Baba. So I shook myself out of sleep and I saw that I was still in my bedroom. Was it a dream? I felt confused. I also felt a lot of love and positive energy in my room, and I felt there was someone next to me. After a few seconds the energy slowly diminished and I no longer felt the presence. For half an hour I felt very positive and that my room had been filled with lots of positive energy. I felt fine. Nothing troubled me anymore.

Bharat bhaiya told me about other devotees receiving dreams from Baba. He said they were real experiences. I still wasn't sure. At the time, as I said, Baba was not coming to Shree because she was expecting Shivam. So when Baba began to give darshan again after Shivam was born I asked Him, "Baba was that you?"

"Which form did you see me in?" His question answered my question. I pray to Him in the form of Shirdi Sai Baba.

11

Not long after that I experienced an inner conversation. I asked myself, if my ex has moved on why shouldn't I? It was the first time I truly asked myself that question.

Again Bharat bhaiya and I went before Baba for darshan, and as usual Bharat bhaiya was the one who asked the questions for me. During the exchange Baba indicated there was someone else for me.

"Who is the guy?" Bharat bhaiya asked.

"I will only tell her when she has moved on," Baba insisted.

I couldn't figure out why He said that.

As they talked I thought, *I wish somebody knew the feelings I am feeling right now.*

At that precise moment Baba looked at me and said, "I can feel your pain."

They continued to talk and Bharat bhaiya said, "So what about her marriage?"

"Look at her," Baba said. "She is perfect. What does he lack in her? She can find a guy who is one in a million. But she has to open up her eyes. The day she will move on she will find that guy in front of her. She will know this guy."

That was the first time Baba gave a clue about my future husband.

Around that same time my mom expressed she was concerned about me. It had been two years since my breakup and my mom went and received darshan from Baba in the South San Francisco mandir.

"When will my daughter get married?"

"I will tell her when she has moved on."

Baba touched my forehead. "She will be fine," and He gave me a flower. When I put that flower on my altar I realized kumkum was coming out of it. Red kumkum. Usually I received flowers with vibhuti in them from Baba.

I asked Inder (Pandher), "What did it mean that I received red kumkum?"

"It could mean, as a single woman," she said, "that you will be getting married soon. Or...that you have a lot of love for Baba."

During the next months I was still grieving over my ex, then finally I came to the point where I said enough is enough. I am going to move on.

The second time my mom went before Baba she asked about me.

"She is ready now," Baba said.

No one knew this! I had just gotten it in my head that it was time for me to move on.

I had darshan with Baba again.

"The guy is right in front of you. There are so many guys around you. Don't you like any of them?"

I said, "No."

"Don't you think anybody is good enough for you?"

"No," I said.

"Allah Malik," Baba replied.

Then Baba explained something to me. "Guys will come and go if you don't move on. Don't look too far. The guy is right in front of you."

I gave it a lot of thought. It really shook me when he basically said 'Guys will come and go and you will still be single.' I could end up wasting my whole life grieving over my ex when he had moved on.

There were many guys in my group. I knew some of them liked me but I didn't feel I liked any of them. So I wrote down the names of the guys I felt had an interest in me, and then I made a compatibility chart; to see who I was most compatible with. Initially my husband, Alok, was not on the list because I was pretty sure he didn't like me. He didn't show any interest. I added his name in the end because I really liked his mom. I loved his mom. I thought his mom was so awesome, and that I would love to have a mother-in-law like that.

His mother came to the US for the first time and I got to see how Alok treated his mother and it came to me, *I would love to have a husband who had so much respect for women.* That's when I thought perhaps I want to marry this guy. I knew other guys liked me but none of them had left an impression on me.

I went to Baba again and there were actually two guys on my mind; one was very spiritually minded. It was so interesting, when I got before Baba it was only one name that I could think of...my husband's name.

"Baba is it Alok?

"Yes, he's the one."

Baba guided me through the whole process. I discovered one of my husband's friends had an interest in me. It was because of that friend that Alok stayed away from me. I also found out that my husband had been in a very trying relationship and as a result, in the beginning, he gave me somewhat of a hard time. Timing, for both of us, was very important when it came to our getting together.

My husband did not approach me. I actually asked Shree about him after darshan one Thursday. "What do I do? This man will not even talk to me?"

Shree told me several things. I thought Baba was still there because of the way she spoke. Then finally Shree said, "Don't worry. He will show his feelings now. You will get married this year. You will marry in the US."

The very next day my husband called me for the first time in my life and asked me out with friends. From that day on he called me every day to talk or to ask me out. I thought, *What happened to this guy?* What turned him around? One month after we started talking we were dating. We married within eight months and his mom adores me.

ANGELA BECTOR

My parents, Jagindar and Chandra Prashad, started attending the South San Francisco mandir. Because I was going through a rough point in my life whenever Baba gave darshan they told Baba about me and they asked questions.

"She is doing her best," Baba told them. "I Am with her."

On one occasion after Baba told my parents He was with me and my family, a vibhuti tika appeared in six framed family photos in my Georgia home. It appeared on my forehead and on my husband's forehead. It looked like someone had blessed us…our photos… with their ring finger. After that I started to pay more attention to what was happening in my house.

Every Thursday when Baba came my parent's would have a message from Baba and I would do what He told me to do as best as I could. Whenever Baba told my parents, "I Am with her," I felt Baba's presence in my house. I would call for Baba and I could actually hear Him walking around.

At night before I went to sleep I could feel His presence. There were also scents that came with Baba's presence. I smelled His hookah, meaning the scent of the smoke, and no one smokes in my house. There were other scents too.

Once I went to bed and about two or three in the morning I felt Him sit right next to me. The bed went down as He sat on it, and I could feel His hand on my head blessing me.

I got more into Baba as a result of my parent's and my experiences associated with South San Francisco. Because of that I began to attend the Shirdi Sai Baba temple in the Atlanta area where I lived at the time.

"If you call Baba with pure love there is no way He is not coming."

ASISH CHANDRA A.KA. ASHU

I was one of the first devotees that were there when Baba started coming. I've seen experiences from early, early on, and have witnessed the transition of what we call our 'Little Shirdi' today.

It's a very magnificent place. There are a lot of things that individuals are not able to grasp because you have to be spiritually ready to experience them. You have your spiritual aspect and then you have Grace. Spiritual aspect means there are things you have to basically earn, and once you do all the earning… Swami's Grace pours forth.

Something I want to emphasize is this: Baba comes here because of the love. People are drawn here because of the love. Whether it's through Amma's (Parvati Lal) service, the love of our sister, Shree… or the love of the children. It is how they embrace the public; it is the love that draws them to the mandir.

From day one Baba has always treated me as if I was different from everyone. He gave me a Hindi title "Sabse Alag". Basically that translates to 'The Separate One"…"The Different One"…"The One Who Is In A Different Category".

Because of Baba's Grace I have been able to see and experience things that people are not able to do on a normal basis. His experiences run through my life like little pieces of a puzzle. They happen whenever and where ever. I don't have to specifically be in the mandir. I can feel Swami's presence. But it's not easy being 'the separate one.' Baba keeps a certain amount of distance between me and others.

The connection between Baba and I, because of His Grace, has resulted in my being able to sense when Baba is about to come. Because I have a strong bond with our sister… Baba… I am able to know. His coming depends on the energy in the mandir. When the devotees are really singing and the energy is high; He comes. It also depends on who is calling Him. There won't be a single bhajan and Baba will come in a snap. It goes back to love again. If you call Baba with pure love there is no way He is not coming. Our sister may be weary because she has been sick, but if someone calls Baba with that kind of pure love…He will come. It is out of her control.

When Baba comes I am physically talking to Him, but my spiritual sense and my mental sense is also communicating with Him at the same time. He basically guides me throughout the process of whatever He wants me to do during bhajans.

It is a part of the Grace. I see myself as His instrument.

Some of the things I do I don't remember. Later when devotees approach me and talk about things that I explained to them or things that I did, I truly don't remember. It is as if … that's what Baba needs to do and I am just an instrument. I surrender my actions to Baba. I don't ask a lot of questions. My mind would be totally cluttered if I tried to remember all the things that happened with devotees who come before Baba. I know everything said at that moment but nothing. Baba prepares us for the work we need to do. Gradually I had to go through a learning phase. As my connection developed with Baba as result of the work, I sometimes know when He's going to ask for something and what he's going to ask for.

Something that I consider to be a wonderful benefit is being able to see Shree's true form. Whether she's in the sister form... the mother form... a Maya form... a Baba form...or an Avatar form. I have seen all her forms and I know who she truly is.

One of my biggest experiences was seeing the Vishwaroop; the same form that Arjun saw in the Bhagavad Gita. Shree and I joke around a lot, but I know when it is her, and when it is not her. That is something many people are not able to recognize.

Shree and I were in a room having a conversation when this happened. We're in the middle of the conversation and she said, "Do you want to see who I really am?"

"What do you mean?" I asked.

"Do you want to see who I really am?" She repeated the question.

I said, "Yeah. Of course I want to see."

"Are you sure?"

"Yes."

"Are you strong enough?" she quizzed.

"Yes."

"Okay."

Snap! We were somewhere else. It wasn't a place with any finite form. I don't know where it was but basically I got to see her Form... how she and Shirdi Baba are one. It wasn't just the bodies. That's the first time I saw their forms as one. Her eyes were His eyes. Her smile was His smile. It was the beauty of Shree and our Sai.

Then Baba decided to take it one step further. He decided to give me a vision of the Vishwaroop. Of course I was going to say yes. Like everybody we've yearned to see God; maybe not everybody, because some people are scared. But I felt like my heart was pure. This was Who I prayed to every day, and He showed me His form. He was one with all the Gods, which is basically everything in the universe. It was all of creation in one. All the religions in one form.

When you think about it, if someone was able to see that and come back into this world… it is a miracle that I was able to come back. There was only a certain amount of time that Baba allowed me to see it because I started shaking. I became scared. He brought me back at that point.

Another experience occurred when Shree and I were having some brother sister time. We decided to go shopping. We were looking for some jeans and we ended up in Express. The jeans we wanted to buy were on a very, very high shelf; basically where they stored the jeans.

"Do you want to see my wings?" she asked as we stood below them.

First I was kind of hesitant. I asked myself, *Do I or do I not?* I was thinking how everybody else was around. Finally, I said yes and suddenly everybody else got blocked out. With her wings she flew up, got the jeans, and came back down. There she stood in front of me as Shree with the jeans. I was worried about what everybody else was going to see, but when you think about Swami's experiences they are always one on one. He is not concerned with the world.

The majority of my experiences with Baba occur in a whole different dimension. It's not always easy for people to grasp that, or to believe it but I am doing the best I can in giving these two examples. There's only so much that I can share with words when it comes to these experiences because they are so intense.

When people come to the mandir on Thursdays I keep emphasizing these are not just murtis sitting there. These are not just statues. They are living. These are entities. When we have bhajans they are living forms. Their clothes become real. They perspire. Their eyes blink. Their hands move. In essence our Little Shirdi gets lifted up to where all the Gods become present. It is a very divine place. It is a very, very powerful place.

What I know is this: you are able to experience Swami just because of the love. If you love Him the belief exist; if the belief exists then the faith builds up; if the faith builds up then anything is possible. Let Love, faith and patience lead the way. He can grant you anything. Have confidence in your love for Swami...in your bhakti. This is not ego. There is no room for ego in devotion. It is simply confidence in your love for Swami. It all starts with that four-letter word, LOVE.

"Baba came immediately. It was almost as if He was waiting for us to come"

DHIREN CHAWLA

From the time I was young I went to see Sathya Sai Baba. A friend of mine told me about the South San Francisco mandir when I was seventeen. That was twelve years ago. I was dealing with some personal issues; that's what drew me to Swami in the first place, and when my friend Nathan told me about South San Francisco I was a little reluctant. Going to see Sathya Sai Baba in Puttaparthi was one thing but I knew very little about Shirdi Sai accept that He had come before Sathya Sai. So I came to South San Francisco questioning the thought that Baba comes through this lady. That was a little 'out there' for me. On my way to the mandir the question *"Why am I going there?"* kept reverberating in my mind. I couldn't get over the fact that I was going to South San Francisco and I didn't know why.

Once I sat down the bhajans began and Swami came. Baba sat on His chair and when He did that I didn't think about

Shirdi Baba. I directed my thoughts to Sathya Sai Baba. I thought, *Swami, I don't know why I'm here, but if you really want me to be here I need to know right now because otherwise I am leaving.* The moment I had that thought Baba pointed to me and called me to Him.

"This place will only help you, if you believe," He said to me.

After He said those words my whole heart dropped... it melted and I did not question in that way ever again.

****

I was going through a sad period, and whatever pain I had I brought to Swami in South San Francisco. At the time someone close to me had drug problems. He had lived on the streets; was in and out of jail and I visited him there. That scenario went on for eight or nine years. When I took Baba's darshan I would ask, "Is he ever going to get better?" It wasn't only me who wanted to know the answer to that question, others in my circle wanted to know.

Baba wouldn't say a lot. He would say, "I am with him. I am taking care of him."

With time he got progressively worst and I went to see him when he was at rock bottom. He had been to see Swami before but he wasn't fully absorbed in Swami. But at that lowest point in his life I felt he fully surrendered to Baba.

I came to the mandir after that visit and I brought a relative of this person. Baba came immediately. It was almost as if He was waiting for us to come. When we were before Him, without any questions being asked, Baba looked at the relative and said, "He is thinking of me right now." He pointed upward with His index finger and said, "This is his last. No more."

I had been coming to South San Francisco for years and

years and years, but I still had disbelief. The question for me was...how can what takes place here...what takes place with Shree be possible?

Not even a week later I went to jail to see him. Without saying anything about Baba I asked him if he had been thinking about Baba at that specific time. He was taken aback.

"I was," he replied.

I told him Baba said, "This is his last time."

As of today that was his last time. Before that when he got out of jail the destructive cycle would begin again. But after Baba announced it was his last time...he got out of jail, began work with this company, met a girl and got married. Now he is a family man with a good life.

SONIA CORTEZ

In 2011 I was very sick; I had surgery and they removed my ovary. Three days after the surgery I went home. I was home for a day and a half and I began to experience a lot of pain in my stomach. I needed to go back to the hospital. My friend, Amanda Pineda, went with me and on the way to the hospital I passed out. I don't remember this but Amanda told me the doctors said I had a lot of water in my abdomen because my intestines were paralyzed. For four and a half days I was in that room in a semi-conscious state. At one point I heard these men, I don't know who they were, talking.

"I don't know why they won't perform another surgery on that lady."

The other responded, "No-no-no-no. If they do two surgeries so close together she will pass away."

The first man replied, "Either way if they don't do another surgery she will pass away because her intestines are paralyzed."

That shocked me. I was shocked. I couldn't speak but I began to move around. I was so nervous and I knew I was moving a lot.

"Call one of the doctors," one of them said. "We need to give her an injection and do some tests but we can't do it with her moving so much."

I began to feel something very hot inside my body. Hot, hot, hot. And I thought, *Oh my God, maybe I am passing away...*but nothing happened. I don't remember what happened directly after that.

Later I attempted to open my eyes because I could hear voices. There was talking, talking, talking. As I began to open my eyes I could barely make things out. I could see shadows but that was all.

"Meera! Meera! Oh my God, thank you! My daughter is here!"

I fully opened my eyes and I recognized my dad. He began to cry and embrace me.

"What happened I said?" very softly.

They read something to me from a hospital paper before my daughter said, "Mom, you spent five days in the hospital."

"Five days???"

"Yes!" she said.

A nurse called a doctor and a doctor came to my room.

"It is good that you woke up, Mrs. Cortez. I was very worried about you," the doctor said. "If you pass a good night tonight, and a good half day tomorrow...you can go home."

I prayed and prayed that day and night. Thank you, Sai Baba. Thank you, Shirdi Baba. Thank you Ganesh for the opportunity, and I went home the next day.

Six months after the surgery my stomach got very large and it was as hard as a stone. I returned to the doctor and he performed some tests. Three days later I received a phone call.

"I'm so sorry, Mrs. Cortez, but I see cancer in your colon."

"What?"

"Yes, and I need to perform another surgery."

"No-no-no," I said and he assured me it was true.

I called Miriam Gomez, and told her what had happened to me.

"Sonia, you pray to Baba," Miriam encouraged me. Then she said, "You know Richard (Selby) and me, we go to South San Francisco. Shirdi Baba is over there. Do you want to go with us?"

I said, "Yes, I want to go." It would be my first time.

When I got to the South San Francisco temple I walked up the stairs inside the house and I began to feel something like electricity going through my body! My first thought was, *'Oh God, maybe I am in the wrong place.'* And I said, *Sai Baba, please help me.*

I saw people sitting on the floor and I told one of the ladies that I could not sit on the floor. She assured me I didn't have to, and she directed me to a chair. I was still questioning if I had come to the wrong place when it was my turn to go up in front of Shirdi Baba. So I said in my mind to Sai Baba, *if I have come to the right place please give me a sign.*

When I was in front of Her...Him, in my mind, I was thinking I want to ask for my house. I wanted to ask Him to save my house. I was thinking of other things, not my stomach.

She gave me the flower and said, "Take this. Your stomach is bad but don't worry."

Oh my gosh. I knew I had not told Him anything. I was in shock. I thought to say something else but She said, "You need to take care of your stomach. Throw this flower in the ocean."

I started crying and took the flower.

After Dick, Miriam and I got back home to southern California, when I was alone, I went directly to the ocean. I said a prayer before I threw the flower. "I was told to do this, and I put this in your hands." With all of my heart and my body I said those words.

Immediately after I threw the flower my body got very hot. That energy went all through my body to the point where my hair stood out from my head. It was full of heat...energy. I looked around and I knew there was no wind, but my hair was standing out from my head.

With that experience I sat down and I cried. I thanked Baba for the second opportunity, and I promised to try to be a good person.

Three months later I was very nervous again when I went to Beverly Hospital to repeat the tests on my condition. I thought *not again. Not again.* When I got there I had a surprise. They changed my doctor. My doctor was American born and now there was an Indian doctor who was scheduled to see me.

"Why are you here?' I asked.

"They changed your doctor," he replied. "Do you know Sai Baba?"

"Why?"

"While you were in the hospital you talked a lot about him, and you said things like 'Om Bhur Bhuva Swaha....' You repeated it and repeated it."

I don't remember any of that.

"Why were you saying that?" He continued. "Have you been to India?"

"Yes," I said, "in 2000 I was in India."

"I recognized those words," the doctor said before he apologized. "And I'm sorry."

"Sorry for what?" I asked.

"I don't know what happened but you don't have anything. Your intestines are clear. You have zero cancer. Come back in five years."

Again I called Miriam and I said this is my story.

Miriam said, "Yes, it is a miracle."

MARIA CRANE

I saw Shirdi Sai Baba in the flesh inside the South San Francisco mandir. I was living with the Lal's in 2008. I had a particular place where I hung out downstairs but basically I slept upstairs on the floor where the mandir is located. It was about midnight and there was no one else in the mandir. Shree used to tease me about my love for Sathya Sai Baba. I would go over to His photo that hung in the mandir and say goodnight to Him every night. That night, as I was saying goodnight, I saw something out of the corner of my eye. I turned and at that moment Shirdi Sai Baba, as a man in the flesh, went and sat on His special chair from which He gives darshan. It just so happens at the same moment Shree was coming up the stairs, and she saw me with my mouth hanging open. I pointed to Baba in the chair. She looked, saw Him and said, "Oh my God! I am getting goosebumps!" It was Shirdi Sai Baba in the body. It was the most stunning thing. He had the cloth on His head...tied around his head. He wore a grayish, whitish gown, more like sacking. They keep Him dressed so decoratively in the mandir but He was not like that. To suddenly see Him live freezes your system. To see Shirdi Sai Baba sitting there live, and not dead, was an unforgettable moment in my life.

****

In 2008, every two weeks we made sandwiches for the homeless. That day it was Bakul Patel, Manav Pandher, Sneha Patel, and I believe Sneha's children were there. We sat together at a table. Manav was at the end and Sneha was across from me. Shree was helping as well. All of a sudden Baba came. He talked about Shree's background in Shirdi; how she was a baby...a little girl ousted and villified because of a disease. It was a bad disease and she was shunned. Baba announced that He had gifts for everybody. He said it was all the dakshina that He collected that day. And then I saw five (5) $100 bills come out of Shree's palm...Shirdi Sai Baba's palm. With each bill Baba would say our full name. Later, where to put that special $100 bill dominated my thoughts. I finally placed it behind a photo of Sathya Sai Baba that I possess to this day. Through a conversation with Shree the following day it was very clear to me that Shree was not in her body when this event took place. She didn't know a thing.

MIRIAM GOMEZ

In August 2010, Dick Selby drove to the South San Francisco mandir from the Los Angeles area where I live. I rode with him, and I invited my friend, Sonia Cortez, to come along. Her doctor had recently found a new tumor in her intestines.

During darshan she received a flower from Baba and some specific instructions about what to do with it.

When I received darshan I showed Him a UPS package.

"What is it?" He asked.

"It's a book about you, Baba. Please bless it."

He did.

Some time later I had a dream. I was walking at Jesus's side, holding Him. I don't understand how I was doing it because Jesus was a very tall, skinny man wearing an almost white robe. At last we took a seat on a bench made of cement.

"Jesus, do you know Sai Baba?" I asked.

Jesus bent forward until His face rested on His knees.

As we sat I continued to talk about how much I love Swami and how much He meant in my life. Jesus didn't say anything, but at a particular moment His face became extremely beautiful and sweet.

That September Dick invited me to go to South San Francisco again. This time it was to celebrate Shirdi Baba's birthday. About three days before the trip I did some editing on a section of my book where I wrote about my first visit to South San Francisco in November 2004.

During that first visit my brother, Livio, my friend, Efrain, and I rode together. After South San Francisco we visited Sacramento and a temple in Colusa where many of Baba's miracles took place. Before we left Colusa out-of-the-blue Efrain asked me who Hanuman was. I gave him a short explanation.

Around three-thirty Sunday morning as Efrain drove us home from Colusa again he asked about Hanuman.

"What is the name of that God who has the head and tail of "Chango"?

Efrain is from Mexico and in folkloric language Chango means monkey. Literally as I answered "Hanuman" my brother, who was seated beside Efrain shouted, "Speed up!" He shouted "Speed up!" because there was a car coming toward us on the wrong side of the street at an excessive velocity! Amazingly… nothing happened! There was no collision.

Afterwards, trembling, Efrain explained, "When I asked you the name of that God as the car headed straight for us, I could see Hanuman in the rear view mirror. He was at the center of a beautiful lotus flower. It was violet in color. I am sure that Hanuman took the car and placed it in a safe place," Efrain remarked, humbly.

I too am absolutely certain that is what happened.

As I took darshan in front of Baba during His birthday celebration I watched His face become the same sweet, beautiful face that Jesus had in my dream! I continued to kneel before Him with nothing being said between us. Then Baba manifested something from the air. He placed it in my hand and it was a beautiful, metal statue of Hanuman.

GURPREET GORAYA

I heard about my wife's (Manava Goraya) experiences with her mom (Shree) in coming to Shirdi in India. She told me as soon as her mom put her feet on the land of Shirdi vibhuti came on her head. Some of the group during a previous visit, including my wife, walked barefeet the entire time they were in Shirdi. I decided to do the same thing when I joined them for a trip.

When we arrived at our hotel I saw my mother-in-law climb the stairs and go into her room. She entered her room and that's when I saw vibhuti was in her hair. We had arrived in Shirdi and there was the vibhuti.

This was my first time experiencing something like this. I thought *Oh my God, is this real? This is the kind of stuff you read about in books, especially in India. You hear about this kind of thing happening back in the1800s...you read about it but you don't hear about it in modern times.*

****

During the second day of my trip to Shirdi, a Thursday; my mother-in-law was very tired. Mommie closed her eyes and laid back to rest on the bed. As she laid there lots of vibhuti formed in her hand. That vibhuti was distributed to everybody.

Shortly after Baba manifested and we explained to the hotel staff what happens with Mommie and Baba. So they gave us a special, private space with a curtain. A photo of Baba hung on the wall.

Baba gave private darshan to all the couples who were present. He blessed us and gave us vibhuti.

MANAV GORAYA

Directly after I graduated from college in 2008, a small group of us attended a cousin's wedding in Canada. Our entourage consisted of my mom, (Shree Lal), Ashu mama, (Asish Chandra) and Justin. (Lal). My mom has lots of family and friends there.

One particular family, who are also relatives, are big Baba devotees. They made consistent trips to South San Francisco on Easwaramma Day, and they would do bhajans for nine hours. Baba always created some kind of miracle for them. We visited that family's home while we were in Canada. The lady-of-the-house had been concerned that she would still be at work when my mom visited but just as Mom entered their mandir the lady-of-the-house joined us.

I walked directly beside my mom as we entered their mandir and all of a sudden Mom turned around, and there was this big earth-tone colored lingam in her hand. It was probably six inches long with a three inch circumference. It had an auspicious eye detail that I recognized. It is the same eye that is on the lingams that were produced out of Mom's mouth.

Currently those lingams line one of the walls of the South San Francisco mandir.

Immediately Mom's body became heavy and she couldn't walk anymore. They sat her down on a couch. After a few minutes they decided she needed to be further away from the mandir or her body would remain in its heavy state. As they helped her walk around some distance from the mandir she felt better.

My mom decided to play around a bit. "I'm not going to go into your mandir because something is going to happen, but just to see...."

She walked over to the entrance and just touched her foot to the line where the doorway began.

"Ooh, I'm in...." and then she stepped back. My mom did not go into the mandir.

Immediately afterwards one of the daughters of the house noticed a large photo of Sathya Sai Baba with both palms raised had fresh, orange vibhuti on it. No one had entered that room.

****

During that same wedding trip we visited the home of Mom's cousin, Krishna. It was late and Baba came. Baba went into Babu's...Krishna's mandir, and Baba swiped His hand through the air all around. Immediately vibhuti appeared on the little murtis and misri...sugar candies, appeared at Ganesh's feet. The entire mandir was blessed.

****

It was Nani's (Parvati Lal) sister, Lakshmi's, birthday, and we were visiting her home during the 2008 wedding trip to Canada. All the cousins were sitting around celebrating. One of the cousin's, Uday Narayan, who had made all the arrangements for the trip and made sure Mom was treated with the greatest of hospitality, was there. In the midst of the celebration, although Mom's face did not change into Baba's, a small murti of Krishna appeared in Her hand. She gave it to Uday.

****

In 2009 we took a cruise to Mexico. Thursday was one of the cruise days and we booked the hall to celebrate Gurupurnima. We brought all of Baba's things with us because He had already said that He would give darshan. It was a special time for a small group of us; lots of family members.

Baba came when we sang kirtans and we dressed Him up. We didn't have carnations as we usually have, but we had roses. Baba explained why He doesn't use roses as a flower to materialize vibhuti and gifts for devotees.

"Roses just fall apart, whereas one carnation I can give vibhuti after vibhuti."

Usually He prefers marigolds, that's His favorite; that flower is readily available in India, but the closest flower that we have in the United States is carnations.

Baba materialized a few lockets and a murti out of the roses.

"I can do it," He explained, "but look, the petals just fall apart."

Normally, after He materializes something for a devotee He gives them the flower in tact, but if He used roses it would simply be a pile of petals.

****

We invited everybody to the house to celebrate Diwali 2006

with the family. Mom was sick at that time. She has been sick for a long time, taking people's pain. After our yearly puja in the mandir we came downstairs to enjoy each other's company, and we began to play antakshari; you sing a song and at the end of the song the consonant that it ends with the next person must start their song with that consonant. We had two teams. The song ended with "D" and immediately Mom started singing, "Deepawali Manayi Suhari" and Baba came. He had everybody sing that song.

"I have already started Diwali for you," He said afterwards. "Out of the tears of my daughter, for the eighteen families that have come here, I have lit eighteen diyas out of her tears."

Baba told us to go up into the mandir to see what was there, and as soon as we went up we saw eighteen lit diyas in a perfect formation...perfect equal distance to each other...perfectly set. I could see it was water, her tears, that were in the diyas. It was not oil and the flames lasted for only our eyes to see. Quickly, we put oil in them. All the families got to keep a diya. There was one per family.

****

It was Easwaramma Day 2010. Family members came from all over Canada to celebrate. Mom was having seizures because she was taking Roshini's pain. She had been having lots of seizures and throwing up blood, something her sister would have experienced if Mom hadn't taken it upon herself. Baba instructed us to pray for my Mom throughout Easwaramma Day in order to continue her life because Mom was severely ill.

The night before the puja we were all sitting around having fun when Baba came.

"I have already started Easwaramma Day for you," He said.

"Go get My water from upstairs."

I ran upstairs to get Baba's water out of the mandir. Nani includes a glass of water with Baba's food when she serves Him on a daily basis. There was no one upstairs but me when I picked up the glass of water at Baba's feet and returned downstairs.

When I arrived with the water Baba said, "I have started the celebration for you. Go! Her life is invested in that diya."

Ashu Mama along with Vijay Nana went upstairs and returned with this absolutely beautiful diya shaped like a Goddess with Her hands extended. They said the diya was sitting in the exact same spot where Baba's water sat. This amazing, lit diya had materialized there.

"This diya is filled with my daughter's tears," Baba informed us.

Once again her tears burned away very quickly so we put oil in the diya.

"Keep this diya lit throughout the celebrations today to continue her life," Baba instructed.

Throughout the celebration that Easwaramma Day we all took turns, three hours at a time, keeping that diya lit.

****

Baba has said Mom's body is special. He said there are others who have manifestations of the Divine but Mom's body is Vishwaroop, meaning any God can come into Her body. I have seen Hanuman come in her body. I have seen Mata come in her body...and of course Baba.

****

Once before Diwali 2012 during Navaratri we were cleaning the house and I heard Shruti (Lal) scream. I was told all of sudden Mom fell on the floor and her tongue extended out of her mouth. Next She began to dance around the mandir.

By the time I arrived and saw Her, like the others I said, "Baba's here! Baba's here!"

Her reply, "No. I am not Baba. I Am Mata."

I became more aware of the manifested red sindoor all over Her head.

"Share this with everybody," were her instructions about the manifested kumkum.

Everyone who was there that day received some of that sindoor.

During that same Navaratri period, my sister, Inder (Pandher), Mom and me embarked on a one day fast for Mata. Instead of nine days we agreed to fast for one day. As we sat together in the mandir, at one point Mom said she was feeling heavy and tired and she lie down. For a moment in time we could tell Mata had come. Her eyes were really big...humongous as she stared at the Durga statue.

"Ask whatever you want...right now," Mata said.

We prayed and touched Her feet and then Mata was gone.

Later I asked Mom, "Do you remember saying, 'Ask whatever you want'?"

"No," she replied. "What are you talking about?"

We had Mata's darshan for maybe thirty seconds that day.

****

Sometimes people have malicious intent. A celebration was being held in 2008. Baba came and I placed a rose garland around His neck. We did not know who brought it. Usually whatever garlands we find in the mandir we place on Baba. He always receives and wears beautiful, hand-made malas from devotees, especially during large celebrations. After I placed the rose mala around Baba's neck He called me forward.

"Do you know who this is from?" He held a portion of the garland in His hand.

"No, I don't know," I replied.

"Why did you put it on me?" He sternly asked before He continued to speak. "Look right here." I saw a tiny puncture on Baba's neck. "I am stung by a scorpion's sting. I will be fine. My daughter will be fine. But whoever has done this should know better. Next time if it's not from you, or you don't know who it is from, don't offer it to Me."

****

Most people have a set way of looking at the world. What rules should be followed...what should and should not be done. I have learned from living with Shree, my mom, that God's view of restrictions is different from man's. Here we have this wonderful woman. She is young. She is beautiful and she has a family. She shows us there is divinity in humanity...divinity within all of us.

NAVEEN GOSWAMI

Around 2008, after doing some shopping I got this urge to simply drop by Shree's house. So I did. I had no plans to go I simply went. Parvati Auntie answered the door.

"Shhhhh. Baba is here," she said.

"Okay," I replied quietly and I followed her inside.

I sat on the sofa where Baba was sitting. A few of Shree's relatives were also there. All of a sudden I felt as if there was this direct connection between Baba and me. Although He was talking with others there was a beam of focused energy on me. The next thing that occurred...I was speaking fluent Urdu! I don't speak Urdu. Baba and I were engaged in a conversation in Urdu...and Shree does not speak Urdu either. I was conscious of speaking in Urdu while it was happening, but I did not understand how I was doing it, nor do I know what I said.

Later my wife, Anita (Bawa), informed me that Shree's chacha had brought a large photo album of Sathya Sai Baba to the house. For some time that day they had been looking through it, and had been deeply engaged in His stories.

****

Through the years, in South San Francisco, Baba has material-ized Shiva lingams and murtis out of His mouth. I have caught more than one of those objects as it came from His mouth. When the objects emerged from Baba's mouth and landed in my hand they were not wet. They were completely dry. It's not like someone could have put it there. I have seen them from the bottom of His throat coming out.

****

I have vibhuti in many places in my puja room. All of the vibhuti came, except for a vibhuti manifestation on a Sathya Sai Baba photo, when Shree was at my house. Every morning I would go to different murtis, pick up some vibhuti and put it on my head...put it on my throat or even eat it. It's a large puja room with vibhuti in six or seven places.

One day Baba gave darshan and this is what He said to me:

"You don't have to take vibhuti so many times. Only one jutki...one pinch is okay from one place. You don't have to go three, four, five, six times."

No one knew that was my daily practice, but Baba knew. He knows what I am doing in my house.

For at least one year after Baba told me that during darshan He teased me on and off.

"Remember! One place. One pinch."

****

At times when I was not feeling well...had a headache, I would receive a call from Shree.

"Bhaiya, are you feeling okay? Do you have a headache?"

Directly after the call I would feel better as if I received a healing just by the telephone conversation. "Especially if I was saying something like. 'Ohhh Baba. Why this headache?'"

That happened more than once.

"Baba promised me five things will happen in my life."

RITA KAUR

I traveled to Shirdi with Shree and about fourteen other people in 2011. We went to Baba's Samadhi and I was the last one in our group to see it. They waited for me outside.

I placed my head on Baba's Samadhi and the next thing I knew a large mala...garland fell onto my arms. *What's that?*, I thought, because it scared me. I opened my eyes and the mala was on my arms. *What should I do?*, I thought. *Should I put this back on the samadhi? Or should I take it?* For one second I thought about it and Baba communicated to me, 'No. You should take this mala with you.'

I hugged the flowers. I kissed them. I almost cried. I walked outside where everybody watied and I gave that mala to Shree Didi.

"Look," I said. "Baba gave me this mala." Everybody put it to their foreheads to receive the blessings.

The next morning they all got up early, around four in the morning, to go to for the aarti. I was very sick and I told them

I didn't want to go. I wanted to go but I just didn't feel like going. I was very sick. Shree Didi decided not to go as well and the two of us stayed in the room.

They left for aarti around 5:30 a.m. and Didi and I could hear the aarti in our room. As we sat and talked on the bed suddenly Didi looked at the door and said, "Baba! Baba! Why are you here? Aarti is going on in the mandir! People are there. Why are you here, Baba?"

Didi's head filled up with vibhuti and Didi became Baba. He sat with one leg up like He usually does. Didi was gone and Baba was there.

I was scared. I was by myself, and Baba said, "Now tell me what you need. Tell me what you want."

"I am very sick, Baba. I am very sick." I said, crying. "I have come to Shirdi. Make me well. I only need a good heart. I have pain in my body."

Baba talked to me for half an hour "Don't be scared. You picked this way. You picked the hard way. Being sick is not easy. But you chose this way. Know I am always with you and nothing can happen to you."

Baba gave me vibhuti. "Drink this vibhuti," He said. "Put it in water and drink it."

Baba also said, "You laid down on me at the Samadhi. Your head was against my head and your hands were on my shoulder. I took the flowers from around my neck and I threw them on you. Those are not normal flowers. They are a pushpa-mala. Take that mala home and dry the flowers. When you see someone who is sick, give them two petals from the mala and the people will be okay. A day will come and there will be no more flowers on the mala, and that many people will come and sit at your feet."

Baba promised me five things will happen in my life. One

promise involved good health and the other involved my son. He will become a doctor.

Then Baba asked me "Can I go now?"

I was scared and crying. I said, "No, Baba."

I didn't know what to say. Should I tell Him yes?

Finally Baba said, "I am leaving now. Take care of my daughter. Give her water when she wakes up and make her lie down on the bed."

Baba hugged me and blessed me. He put His hand on my head and there was vibhuti on his hand so there was vibhuti on my head.

When Didi woke up she didn't remember anything.

She looked at me and said, " Hey, there's vibhuti on your head."

"No," I said. "There is vibhuti on your head. Baba came. He blessed me and there was vibhuti on His hand. That's how I got vibhuti on my head."

I told her everything that happened and when everybody returned from aarti I told them that Baba came.

Manav (Goraya) said when she was standing in the line at the mandir she thought about us. She said she thought, *We are all here at the mandir and Rita is with mom and Baba will be there with her.*

Later when I discussed what happened in Shirdi with Didi, she said she was going to ask Baba if what I said about the pushpa mala was true. So Didi asked Baba about the mala. Baba told her yes it is true.

****

Around 2010 Didi came to my house for the first time and vibhuti came on Baba's picture. The second time she came maybe sixteen people were sitting in my living room. Didi sat on my sofa. I got one of my dining room chairs and sat directly in front of her.

She asked, "Why are you sitting there?"

"Because I want to see your face," I said.

We all talked for maybe twenties minutes and suddenly she was staring at me. I was sick at the time and I thought it was Baba so I was a little scared, but I kept laughing and talking. Next Didi started acting like she was going to throw up. She pointed her first finger at me and said, "Come. Come."

I knew she wanted me to hurry. I didn't know what was happening but I put my hands in front of her mouth. The next thing I heard was a kind of click behind her teeth. Something hit her teeth and a Lakshmi Mata murti came from Her mouth. It dropped into my hand. It was made of metal.

She sunk down onto the sofa and

Justin (Lal), Alicia (Lal) and everybody gathered around her. She was cold and I ran to get her a blanket. After covering her we all examined the murti.

When Didi woke up she gave instructions as to what to do with it. "Wash it in milk and water. Put rice on it and beneath it and put it on the altar."

Didi visited my home several times and the majority of the times vibhuti manifested somewhere in my house. Throughout this time I have dreamed of Baba and He has told me things that have come true. I have talked to Didi about these dreams. Baba says He can come in any form, any time.

MALINI KESHAVAPRASAD

I got connected with the South San Francisco mandir through a friend of mine in California. His name is Rattan Naidu. He telephoned my husband who had just arrived in Connecticut from Puttaparthi.

Rattan asked, "Hey. What are you doing in Connecticut? Come here to California. You can see Baba."

At the time I told them I had experienced so many things with Baba in Puttaparthi that I was content. But I knew my husband would go crazy to see Baba's miracles anywhere and everywhere. Soon after that phone call he took a flight to California and Rattan took him to the mandir.

Rattan, his wife and his children were musical people; they were singers so they sat down front. My husband didn't know anyone in that group. He only knew Rattan and these were not your usual Sathya Sai people. The majority of the people were from Fiji and my husband wasn't a singer, so he sat all the way in the back of the bhajan hall. It was my husband's very first experience in the South San Francisco mandir, still, when Baba came in trance through Shree Baba, He walked all the way to the back where my husband sat and looked directly at him.

"Doctor, come and sit in front."

You see, my husband was so accustomed to sitting in front on the Puttaparthi veranda! Immediately my husband knew *This is Baba. Who else would know?*

Who would have known that he was a doctor? Rattan did not introduce him as a doctor.

Baba materialized the vibhuti for him from a carnation flower, and then he took another carnation flower and materialized the vibhuti and said this is for your wife. This happened on Tamil New Year's Day.

After bhajans was over and everyone had gone downstairs, after resting Shree finally came down. Again she looked at my husband. This time he said she seemed to be asking for water or something and she looked like she was choking. My husband didn't know what to do. By the time he could react, a lingam from her mouth came out. My husband caught it. By that time someone else brought Shree some water.

My husband was new to this place, and he was shocked by the whole thing. So when he came back to Connecticut with all these experiences he told me definitely you have to go.

I came to the South San Francisco mandir for the first time in June of that same year. I saw Shree for the first time before bhajans began. Everybody was still downstairs waiting for the puja to start.

My friend, Lakshmi, pointed to this lady and said, "This is Baba."

She was pointing to Shree. Here is a young lady pointing to another young lady saying, "This is Baba." I just stared. I was shocked.

After Lakshmi said that, Shree looked at me with a strong stare. It was a confident look. Then she commanded the people around, "It is time for bhajans. All the people who are interested in singing can go upstairs."

As soon as she said that, immediately something happened in me. I felt I was taken back to my interview in Whitefield with Puttaparthi Baba in 1996. That time Baba had called my family for an interview and during that interview, Baba looked at me and then said, "All singers go upstairs." Immediately my mind went to that incident! I felt transported to that time.

During the bhajans I had experiences when Baba came while Shree was in trance. I knew from the beginning that this is the same Baba. It was very thrilling for me. I saw the energy as Baba but it was through his leelas...Shirdi Baba...a Female Form.... But I knew it was the same Baba.

For both of us, who had lived so close to the Puttaparthi Baba from 1992 to 2006, we knew this was the same Baba. We lived there for thirteen and a half years. Having morning darshan and evening darshan. Such a close proximity, and for us to experience Baba in a different set up... in a different form not even Baba in His robe as we had come to know Him.... It was with His grace that we were able to get that knowledge. How else would we have understood?

BHARAT KONA

I was more of an agnostic for most of my life. As I grew up I enjoyed going to temples and doing traditional pujas with my parents, but that was more culturally based than religious or spiritual. Even in college I went to temples more as a tradition than faith. It was around the late nineties when I started hearing about Shirdi Sai Baba. I presumed it was another fad occurring in India and did not pay attention to what was said, and when I came to the US my temple visits became less and less.

In early 2007 I visited a school friend on the east coast. I've known him since 1992 and he was a bit of an agnostic like me. During our conversation one day he kept talking about Sai Baba and miracles. I would have generally brushed it off, but this individual is someone I know who is very rational, and on top of that he is a computer science professor at a well-known university. His comments made me think about Sai Baba and also divinity in general. Time passed and several things happened that deepened my interest in Sai Baba.

One of my long-time good friends in the Bay area mentioned a Sai Baba temple in South San Francisco. He spoke about Sai Baba speaking through an individual and miracles happening in the temple. By then, I was so curious and very much ready that I went to the temple the next Thursday.

I arrived a little late and Baba was already there. I saw this person sitting in a big chair up front but I didn't know it was Baba until the friend who invited me, Rao Pasumarthi, told me so. During those days Baba used to walk around when He gave darshan and when He came to me I don't know what happened to me but I touched His feet. This is not something I would normally do. Even as a child and all the times I had been to temple I never thought touching the feet was the right thing to do. But my first time with Baba in South San Francisco, I touched His feet. After that He gave me a flower. I looked into the flower and saw there was vibhuti there. Rao told me to keep the flower in my home along with my other idols where I did puja, and I did exactly that. At the time I didn't know what I thought about this Sai Baba, but the next day when I prayed at home I saw there was more vibhuti in the flower. The amount of vibhuti increased even more by the following day. For at least two months a little vibhuti continued to come in the flower Baba gave me.

****

Over time I have experienced many miracles in the South San Francisco temple, including manifestations of vibuthi, miniature idols, etc. In addition, I have experienced Sai Baba answering questions in my mind and predicting future events in my life. All of the predicted events through Sai Baba at the temple have come true.

One of the most significant events was this:

I was looking for a new job in mid-2008 and was primarily interested in joining a good startup in the San Francisco Valley as I never worked for a startup before. After a few weeks of searching I found one very good startup in my field of technology. I applied for a couple of positions online and also reached out to my contacts to help me connect with the hiring managers. Despite my best efforts nothing happened. Meanwhile, I got calls and interviews at other companies.

One Thursday I took a printout of the jobs that I applied for at the startup company to the South San Francisco mandir. I showed it to Baba and asked Him to help me get a job there. Without even looking at the printouts Baba said very emphatically, "Only at that company will you get a job."

I was delighted and thanked Baba.

The next day was Friday and I was optimistic that I would soon get a call for an interview from the startup company. To my surprise I did get an email on that day, but not what I expected. The email indicated that the job was filled with an internal candidate. I was terribly disappointed but thought that Baba's words would never go wrong. I kept thinking about it through the weekend and I wanted to ask Baba about it on the next Thursday.

On the following Monday, to my pleasant surprise, I got an email from the same company asking me if I was interested in a second job. I realized I had applied for two jobs at that company and I was called for the 2nd job. Later I learned my resume was somehow forwarded to the hiring manager for the second position, who till then had not received my resume through the other sources. After I responded I was scheduled for an interview on Thursday of that week. My interview was at a coffee shop and was very informal. I knew by the end of the interview that I would get an offer.

That evening I went to the mandir for bhajans.

"How is your job search going?" Baba asked with a smile when I went up for darshan.

"It is going very well and Your words are coming true," I said with deep gratitude.

The very next day I got the call from the hiring manager and he made a verbal offer. By Monday morning I had the written offer in my hands. It was unbelievable that I got the offer three days after the interview. Prior to that, for weeks, I attempted to get an interview at that very same company. I accepted the offer and I had wonderful time at that company.

I remember this experience very vividly even after the years and have nothing but gratitude for Sai Baba who continues to support me in every single way.

****

During the times Baba came after bhajans He taught about the world, divinity...many things. The teachings weren't elaborate. They were more like parables based on the worldly things people continuously asked Him for. "Why do you people ask Me for those things? I Am willing to give you much more than that." "Nothing is permanent here." He spoke of human desire...so many things He spoke of. He would tell you if you needed to change your ways because He knew what you were doing in your daily life, and He encouraged individuals to get on the right path.

****

I strongly encouraged my parents, Chalapati Rao Kona, my dad, and Surya Prakasam Kona, my mom, to go and see Shree in Shirdi, India while she was there in 2011. I believed it might be their opportunity to see Baba in Shree in His full form, or in some aspect of that. At first they encountered problems securing transportation to Shirdi, but then all of a sudden something opened up and they were able to go. While they were there they saw and spoke to Shree, and they told me they saw vibhuti coming out of her head on multiple occasions. They also saw Baba when He came, but they were clear they saw vibhuti coming out of Shree's head even when Baba was not there.

****

In 2011 I told my cousin sister, Visala Kona, who lives in India, about Shree and the South San Francisco temple. She asked me to please let her know the next time Shree was going to India because she wanted to meet her, and perhaps get to see Baba. Visala is a very devoted Sai Baba devotee, and when I told her Shree had plans to travel to Shirdi in 2012, she took my mom to Shirdi so they could meet Shree there.

Visala and my mom planned to be in Shirdi for two days, and they managed to be there at the same time Shree and several of her family members were there. For some reason when Baba came through Shree at a temple on the first day; my mom and cousin weren't there. Before they left Shirdi the next day they saw Shree and her family. During the meeting they were told how Baba had come and gone the day before. Shree told Visala she was sorry, and that she thought Baba would come again but He didn't.

Visala felt very bad after hearing this and she began to talk to Baba. She stressed how she wanted to see Him. After listening to Visala Shree said she would take Visala's prayers to Baba, but Visala kept insisting she wanted to see Baba. At some point she started to cry. Believe it or not after awhile Baba came back into Shree, and He gave darshan to the group that had gathered. The first person He called for darshan was my cousin sister. Baba called her by her full name; a name that even I had forgotten. He allowed her to ask questions. Visala said the majority of the answers He gave have come true. The other answers...there is still time.

Visala was emotionally overwhelmed by that experience for a long time. She has cried and thanked me over and over again during phone calls from India. I told her it was her bhakti that made it happen.

AJAY KOTHA

I was looking for a mandir when we discovered the South San Francisco mandir. One of my wife's friends gave us the information and I actually read some things about it on the internet too.

The first time we had darshan of Baba there, he manifested a standing Ganesha for us. At first I didn't know why Baba manifested that particular idol. After a while I realized, a long time ago my great-grandfather had found a Ganesha and actually built a small mandir for it. To this day devotees still visit that mandir, and I believe Baba manifested that Ganesha for us because He knew, long time ago, my great-grandfather found a standing Ganesha in a canal and built that mandir.

****

In 2011 I told Shree, who I call Didi, that I wanted to go to India for a visit. At that time it was tough to get a H-1B stamp. Many people warned me about how tough it was, but regardless of the things they said I booked tickets to India and I made an appointment with the VISA office on a Thursday.

When I went for the appointment the representative asked for a certain document that I did not have. I knew I didn't have it so I started chanting the Tryambakum and I began to give him one wrong document after another. I knew they weren't the right documents but I was giving them to him anyway. After seeing all those documents and saying "Not this. Not this". He finally asked me some questions and he let us go.

NARENDRA AND SWARNALATHA KOTHAKOTA

My wife, Swarnalatha, was having health problems. We went to Kaiser and the doctor prescribed some medication to reduce one of the symptoms, but it did not help. They told us to be patient, but even after we allowed time to pass there was no improvement.

One day during darshan at the South San Francisco mandir Baba called my wife up for a personal darshan. He had never called her before. Baba only calls when the devotee requires it and he is having pain. I didn't go up. She went up alone and Baba spoke to her. After He spoke to her she starting crying and went downstairs where everyone gathers after bhajans. I asked her what was wrong. She said Baba told her the problem could only be solved with an operation.

We went back to Kaiser, changed the doctor and sought a second opinion. She ended up having a pathology test and the report made her condition, adenomyosis, very clear. The first diagnosis was incorrect, and because of that report the doctors determined the only solution was surgery.

We chose a date and before the day of her surgery my wife had Baba's darshan. He gave her a flower.

"Don't worry. I will be with you during the surgery," Baba said.

We asked the doctors if Swarnalatha could take the flower with her into the surgery room and they allowed it. After the surgery she was fine.

KANWAL LACHER

I have full faith in the vibhuti for everything...I use it for all hurdles in my life.

In December 2012 I took my car to the dealer because my parking light was out. Earlier that day my seatbelt buckle broke, and in the process of getting the parking light repaired the dealer told me my seatbelt needed replacing. The light cost $137.00 and they wanted over $300.00 to repair the buckle. I told them not to fix the seatbelt.

When I arrived home I said to Baba, "I have full faith in vibhuti," and I told my daughter, Geet, to go inside and get vibhuti from my puja room. When she gave it to me I sprinkled Baba's vibhuti on the seatbelt buckle and on the dashboard. Everything works perfectly now.

****

It was during Diwali 2011 and Shree called me on the telephone. At the time I didn't know Baba sometimes called devotees on the phone. So when Shree called I told 'her' about a

$480 traffic ticket I received when I attended bhajans.

"I was coming to your house and coming to the mandir and look at what I got? Why did I get a ticket?" I asked.

"Throw the ticket in the garbage," 'she' said.

"I don't want to go to the jail," I said to her.

Later I came to the understanding it was Baba talking.

He just laughed on the phone after I mentioned jail.

"Do the Hanuman Chalissa every day when you pray," He advised.

"Ok, " I said, and I started doing the Hanuman Chalissa.

I received a letter from the city. They wanted to verify that it was me who got the ticket. I replied telling them it was. Here it is two years later and I never received anything from the city again.

ALICIA LAL

I started coming to the mandir in 2008, that's when I started dating Justin (Lal). To be honest it was a little nerve-racking, coming to a whole new house under those circumstances. During those days it was really packed for bhajans. Every Thursday there were nearly 400 people. I didn't come all the time because I was simply dating Justin. Once again to be totally honest, when I started coming to bhajans alone, I wasn't really paying much attention to Baba. I came to hang out with Justin. I never knew anything about Shirdi Sai Baba, or Baba in general. When it came to praying I would go to a mandir and pray to all the Gods as one. So when I came to the South San Francisco mandir and heard how Baba said "All Gods are one," I thought, *Oh my God. I believe I know where I belong now.* I was deeply touched by that in 2010.

After that I began to sit closer to the front during bhajans. Before I always sat in the back but after that I felt closer to what was unfolding in the mandir so I sat closer to the front. Baba would always look at me...look straight at me and I would feel a little bit uncomfortable. I would check my thoughts at that moment because I felt he knew what I was thinking. Whenever I went up before Baba for personal darshan I would just touch His feet. I wouldn't say anything. Baba would talk to me. He would talk to me about Justin, and it was from those things that Baba said to me that in my heart I felt I had found someone, outside of mom and dad, who is listening at all times.

That was a very stressful year and I decided to do the Vrat puja. I believe I was one of the first people in the mandir to do that puja. Justin questioned my ability to do it. "Can you do it?" he asked.

"I can do it," I said. "For Him… For Baba I can do it."

Every Thursday I woke up at 5 a.m. and I did everything I could. At the end of the puja when I went before Baba He told me I did something wrong. When He told me what it was; it concerned a song I sang improperly, He was totally right! It was weird that He knew that I had sung that song in that way. From that point on I was sure He was with me at all times.

****

Someone told me that there was this wonderful smell that came from my mother-in-law's feet. Most people believe the jasmine smell comes on Thursdays when Baba comes, but actually it's there on a daily basis.

One day she was sitting at my house and Inder asked me, "Have you ever noticed how mom's feet smell like jasmine flowers?"

"No," I said. "I've never gone and smelled Mom's feet."

Mom always wears an ankle bracelet around her ankle, and I asked, "Can I…?"

"What?" She asked before she understood and gave me permission.

And then I smelled it. Even that day she was just sitting

there looking at television and the smell was very strong.

****

We were travelling in India and we bought a murti of Shirdi Sai Baba while we were in Shirdi. In the airport from Shirdi to Mumbai things went perfectly fine. We went through the security checkpoints without any problem.

One night we were all lying down in Mumbai. It was pin drop silence in the room. All of a sudden there was this loud, loud noise. Something had dropped to the ground. Everybody woke up and I thought, *'What is that?'*

There was glass shattered everywhere.

The first thing Justin said was, "Oh my God...don't tell me."

"What?" I asked.

"Did the murti fall?"

We looked up where the box had been sitting, then down on the ground. The murti had fallen. We opened the box and Baba's head had broken off!

Everyone was crying. How could this have happened? I yelled at Justin and asked him how. We were all trying to figure out how the murti had fallen when Baba came. Baba was quiet and He looked like He had a lot of tension around His head.

We cried and apologized to Baba. We didn't know what was going to happen! Baba put His leg up like He sits all the time and He looked at Justin.

"Come here," He said.

He spoke one on one with Justin.

Then He called me. He told us my dad (Jagindar Prashad) was supposed to pass away that night! I started crying. I didn't know what to say.

"I took it," Baba said.

91

It was very hot there and with all the partying activity the night before Baba also told us Justin's life was in jeopardy. That Justin was simply not going to wake up that next morning.

I cried even more because I would've lost Justin and my dad. I reached out and held Baba's feet. "I don't know what to say to You, Baba." I thanked Baba so deeply.

He looked at me, "When we go back I'm going to make you Gurumukh."

I wasn't really familiar with what becoming a gurumukh meant.

We glued Baba back together as best as we could because we felt there was something very powerful about that particular murti. Many people said we should just leave it there, but we put it together and put it in a box. We wanted to take that particular murti with us.

We were going through the Dubai airport security check when they stopped us. They believed there was a gun inside Baba's murti. The shadow image inside the murti actually looked like a gun. I was freaked out. I think Baba was testing us defense wise to see what we would say if someone said we were putting a gun in our God. On the screen you could see the image looked exactly like a gun!

After they saw the image they brought the guards out with their guns.

"There's a gun in here and we are going to break it open," they said.

"You're not going to break this open," I replied. "We went through all these other airports and there was no problem."

"Shut up," he said but I kept talking.

"We would never put a gun or anything of that sort inside of our God. Would you put a gun in your God?" I asked. "Would you smuggle something inside of your God?"

Justin showed them the tattoo of Baba that he had just gotten on his arm. They said it was a picture of Justin. They did not believe us.

Usually I am not so talkative, especially in front of Justin's mom but that day I told them off for Baba.

"How dare you accuse us of such a thing? No matter what you say we are taking this murti back to the United States. I don't care if you like it or you don't. But you are not going to break this murti open. You can go ahead and arrest all of us."

Well...we got through that security check with the murti.

When I had darshan of Baba in the South San Francisco mandir Baba brought that up to me.

"I think you are a very smart person. There was a moment when I heard the things you said."

Justin was next to me. "Oh my God. I think He is talking about what happened in Dubai."

"I love you from My heart," Baba continued. "If nobody is there for you...I am there for you. Even if this guy does not do right by you, I will do everything I can to make sure he sees he has made a mistake. You showed everybody that they made a mistake believing they saw something that was not there."

Baba made me Gurumukh that Gurupurnima, and I was the happiest person you can imagine.

****

Once while Justin and I were driving home from Sacramento, California we saw Baba walking along the highway. We both saw Him. Baba was wearing his dhoti and carrying His sack. Justin and I were actually arguing at the time. It was like He was reminding us that He is always with us. Because we saw Baba we started talking about Baba. From that point on we talked about Him the entire way home.

JUSTIN LAL

The mandir was much smaller when I was around eleven years old. That's when things first started happening with my mom. She was just sitting in the front of the room. All of a sudden we could smell all this vibhuti. It was all around. We all noticed it and we started asking, "What is that smell? Where is it coming from?"

I noticed my mom's facial structure changed somewhat. Not like how Baba comes today. Not like that. Her face looked very peaceful, and suddenly the top of her head was just covered with vibhuti.

My first reaction, as an eleven-year old boy, was, *Oh my God, this is weird! I can't ever tell anybody. Especially not my friends.* After a couple of years I got over the fact that this kind of thing happens to my mom.

When things first started my mom didn't know what was happening. It started after my mother took a trip to India to see Baba, Sathya Sai Baba. At the time she had a brain tumor; was totally bedridden with memory loss. My mom didn't remember any of us. Me. My grandmother.... My dad and I would just sit in the room with her and pray.

My grandmother took Mom to Puttaparthi and Baba gave her an interview. During that interview Baba put his hand on her head; she came back and went to the doctors and there was no tumor. Nothing. That's when my mom started believing more. After that she started believing more in miracles and she leaned more toward Baba. She became real close. She was devoted all the way. My mom prayed a lot. A lot.

One of my earliest memories of the manifestations that came from Baba was the sugar candy that He manifested. In the beginning it wasn't so much pendants and things like that. It was sugar candy. Some of them were huge; perhaps three inches tall and they manifested from a flower. At times Baba's garlands were full of sugar candy.

Over the years I have watched my mother take on more and more sickness. It has increased with time. From seizures to heart attacks to just normal pain; there is always something different. I keep my faith in Baba through all of this because I know things will be okay; that my mom will be all right. Even though it hurts at that time to see my mom go through it, I know He will take care of it and this episode too will pass.

****

My dad used to always play the doluk. One day he had to be somewhere and he couldn't play. I picked up the drum and started playing. Everybody said you play better than your dad. From that day forward I never put it down. Afterwards when Baba came I told Him, "This is something I want to do. I want to play doluk. I like it. I enjoy it." And I guess that was His gift to me. Now many times when I sing during bhajans and play doluk for Baba a flower falls. I have also noticed it is at the time when I am singing that Baba usually chooses to come.

****

We went to Shirdi with my mom. It was about twenty of us at the train station. This old guy, who looked like a beggar, came up to Uday (Narayan) and me. "Will you buy me some tea?" he asked. We thought he was going to ask for money but he didn't. So we bought him some tea and crackers, and he said he wasn't going to eat anything unless it was in his bowl. He dug this bowl out of his backpack, put His food in his bowl and squatted and ate right there. Uday's daughter came running up and the man said, "Oh you're a little Mata," and he dug in his bag and gave her a small rudraksh. "Here's a little gift for you." After that Uday gave him Rs.500 and said something like, 'You're going to need this' before he walked away. So I decided to give him some money too. I gave him money and I turned around and spoke to someone else. The next thing I knew he tapped me on my shoulder and said, "You will need this more than I will," and He gave the money back to me. I was shocked. I went to call Uday to tell him what just happened and by the time I came back the man was gone. I knew that was not just a beggar. We boarded the train and rode through another city. As we rode through that city we saw the exact same man walking. When I told my mom about Him she just smiled and didn't say a word. I know that was Baba.

PARVATI LAL

We we're a very poor family in Fiji. My husband, Ram Lal and I had two daughters. Roshini, who was born handicapped, and Malthi…Shree, born January 19, 1969.

Roshini was premature and after she finally came home from the hospital I tried all kinds of things to help her. Medicines. Massage. Church. But nothing worked. I had heard of Sathya Sai Baba and one day I picked up our local newspaper and there was a picture of Him inside. I don't know what was going on in my mind at the time but after I saw the photo I decided to cut it out and frame it. It was a small picture of Baba. I had never seen a photograph of Sathya Sai in the newspaper before, and never saw one after that.

After I framed His picture I started doing special prayers to Him every Thursday and wouldn't eat meat on Thursdays. Everybody continued to eat meat but I would not. So Thursday was Baba's day and Monday was Shiva's day. As time passed my mind was always on Baba, and I began to believe in Him deeply. One thing I prayed to Baba a lot about was Roshini, and after I began to pray to Him I noticed little changes began to happen. Roshini started talking and laughing, and I thought, *Ohhh, these prayers to Sathya Sai Baba are working.*

Four or five years passed and during that time some people talked badly about Baba. They said bad things about how He looked...His big hair. But I continued to believe in Sathya Baba no matter what they said. It was in this environment that Shree grew up.

When Shree was around ten years old I noticed whenever she was relaxing in the house, just sitting on the floor, on the couch, or the family was fixing hair, her face would change. My parents would say, "Look at Shree's face," and because of how she looked people made fun of her. They would laugh and tease us about her face. They said she looked like a monkey. Nobody took what was happening to her seriously. Some said perhaps she was being bitten by a mosquito and had swollen up because of the bite, but I didn't know what was happening to my daughter. She looked like Hanuman to me. It was all red like Hanuman's face. I worried a lot because of this.

During that time Shree would go to school and they would pick on her, and then there would be fighting, and I was angry too because of what was happening. Yet she continued to receive and give lots of love inside the family. Some of them said there was too much love in Shree and that was why this strange thing was happening to her.

About a year later, in 1983, I decided to move to the United States for Roshini's sake. I felt she would receive better health care. By then I had a large mandir in my home with a big photo of Baba, but I left all of that and kept the small photo of Baba I cut out of the newspaper in my purse.

We made the journey to the States. When I stood in the customs line in the Los Angeles airport I felt some fear. I was afraid because I felt like a stranger. I thought *Who is going to help me here?* As I was feeling this way inside I heard Baba say, "Don't worry. You go. I Am here." I was strengthened by that.

As I stood in that line Roshini began to throw up and a custom's officer called me forward. I was frightened when he called me because I didn't know what it meant. The next thing I knew he had stamped my VISA for a six month stay. "You go," he said, and immediately I knew it was Baba.

Then he looked at me just like Baba, and he asked, "You okay?"

"Yes," I said.

"Okay, my child, then go."

That's how Shree and my family came to California. Once I got here I took nurse's aide caregiver jobs, and no matter where I went I took Baba's photo with me. I chanted His name from the time I woke up, during work, and before going to bed at night.

In 1984 we rented a one bedroom house. We started a mandir with my small photo of Baba, and began to hold bhajans every Thursday. We always served a little food afterwards. In the beginning there were four people who joined us for bhajans. Right away vibhuti started coming on the small photo and when I called home to Fiji I was told vibhuti had also started coming on the large picture of Baba that I left behind.

More time passed and we bought the house where the mandir is today. Baba started coming into Shree's body in 1997, and already vibhuti was coming in the mandir. After Baba started coming into my daughter, changes were taking place on a daily basis. Sometimes there would be vibhuti in her hair, sometimes kumkum and more and more people began to come for bhajans. The people would come to Baba with their sicknesses...leukemia...this...that, and after so many came with their sicknesses my daughter began to be sick. If someone was in the hospital, in ICU, or for other reasons, if an IV was in their arm, my daughter would be sick and while she looked to be sleeping she would talk about what was being done to that person in the hospital. While she was talking to us, my daughter was experiencing the IV or whatever else was being done to the person. Sometimes you could see the evidence on her body.

****

One day, in 2010, I got a phone call from Justin, my grandson, that his mom was going to be taken to the hospital in an ambulance. I told him I would meet them there. Naveen Goswami agreed to take me, and just so happened we ended up directly behind the ambulance as it drove to the hospital. When we arrived the ambulance doors opened up and my daughter was suddenly okay; from what appeared to be a heart attack to suddenly okay...but she was very different.

This started a period of time, which many people still do not believe and others refuse to believe, but what I am sharing is true. My daughter's body was there but it was not my daughter...and it was not Baba. From the beginning I knew something had changed because of how she reacted to me, Justin and Naveen. Even when she arrived home after she was quickly released from the hospital, my daughter had to become acquainted with our place and her own belongings. This went on for several days. She acted differently; did everything very fast...and she did everything! The house...shopping...everything.

Finally, one day early in the morning Baba came. One of the children came to get me because He wanted to speak to me in private.

Baba was sitting on Shree's bed. I went to sit down.

"Close the door," He said.

I closed the door.

"There is something I am going to tell you if it is the right time or not. I am telling you, Parvati, everything." Then Baba said. "This is not your daughter. Your daughter is already gone."

I started to cry and cry.

"Don't cry," Baba said. "Her time was up. The body is Shree but inside is Maya. Not your daughter."

I continued to cry as I listened.

"Sorry," He told me. "Shivam is coming now. But don't worry. I am taking care of everything. Your daughter has been taken to Brahma-loka and is being cared for. Now, here in her place, is Maya."

Maya was the one who had been living in my house from the time Shree arrived at the hospital. I worried how long Maya would stay.

I have had so many experiences with my daughter. So-o many. But this one.... My life changed a lot when Baba started coming to Shree.

****

For a long time I have loved Sathya Sai Baba. In 2011, when He was in the hospital, before He passed away I cried so much for Him. I couldn't believe what was happening. Shree was very sick during that time, but I didn't relate her sickness to Sathya Baba. She was so sick for one week that Anand and Geetha Nuggenhalli spent the night. She talked as she lie in the bed in a way that I didn't understand about IVs and doctors. She constantly talked about someone being sick.

Who's sick? I wondered, and then she mentioned something about curly hair and I said, "Ohhh, Sathya Baba!"

This is what Shree had been talking about.

The next day Anand and Geetha were sitting with her in the bedroom. I came upstairs.

"What is happening?" I asked my daughter.

"Amma, I am very sick," is what she told me.

Knowing what she had been through during the week and seeing her at that moment I started talking directly to Sathya Baba. I was so concerned for my daughter. I knew she was experiencing what Sathya Sai Baba was going through in the hospital. I cried to Him because it is very hard for me to see my daughter in such pain. I told Him I know that you are doing everything but I wanted Him to spread some grace on Shree.

After a short while she looked like she was going to sleep. I was relieved that she could rest. Geetha, Anand and I talked and then Shree woke up and said she was going to take a shower.

"Good. You shower and I will go cook." I needed to prepare to go to Jagindar Prashad, Justin's father-in-law's house. Next thing I know Anand came running.

"Auntie! Auntie!"

"What is it?"

"Baba is coming!"

We both rushed up the stairs. I focused on Sathya Baba's big picture that hung in the mandir.

"Auntie," Anand said, "don't look at Baba's picture. Baba is here!"

I looked and Sathya Baba had come through Shree. She walked and acted like Sathya Baba with His hands behind His back. Even her hair was curly.

I burst into tears.

"My child...my child," Baba said to me. "Don't cry. I Am here. I Am looking for you to say good-bye. I Am going...but I Am always here. "

We all cried before Baba got back into bed.

I left and spent time at Justin's father-in-law's home. When I returned to my house at 7:00 o'clock I was with Shree when she made some unusual breathing sounds before her head dropped. Minutes later my nephew, Uday Narayan, called and told us to turn on the TV because Sathya Sai Baba passed away. Directly after that, after a week of being gravely sick, Shree sat up in the bed and said, "I am hungry, Amma. Give me some tea."

****

I had been having trouble with my leg for a long time. Baba told me, when He came to Shree, that I would have to have surgery, but not to worry that He would be with me. Surgery time came in 2012. At some point on the day of my surgery Shree asked Baba to give her my pain.

They took very good care of me in the hospital before they prepared me for my operation. This doctor came and talked to me right before they wheeled me into the operating room. Right before he put on his surgical mask the same doctor came to my bedside, "I am operating on you. Are you okay?" he asked.

At that moment, when I looked into his face it was Baba! It was Baba's face that I saw! I recognized Baba! Moments later the anesthesia started to work and I had my surgery. Baba was the one who operated on me.

After I was released from the hospital Shree told me she had asked Baba to give her my pain for two days; for two days I had no pain. I slept very well. On the third day Shree told me the pain would return to me, and ohhh my goodness the pain. My pain returned to me.

"When these bouts of sickness come on Shree she's never scared. At that time she is thinking about others."

SANJEEV MASON

I believed deeply in Shirdi Sai Baba before I came to the United States from London. I never planned to come to the US, but as my long-distance relationship developed all of a sudden things worked so smoothly for me to make a visit. I was aware that Baba came through Shree but to witness it was something else altogether.

When I first met her Shree was very sick. When Thursday arrived and bhajans were scheduled she was still very sick. But when Baba gave darshan… He was not. Not only was He not sick, He could go up and down the stairs, bend and do many things Shree simply could not do. Baba even danced. It was amazing.

****

Over several Thursdays I watched Baba come and give darshan during bhajans. Out of my love and reverence for Baba I decided to clean the whole temple. Soon after I completed the work Shree came up to me. "You've done a good job."

At least I thought it was Shree until she said, "This is for you." She opened her hand and suddenly there was a Shivalinga in it. I knew there had been nothing in her hand and I must have hesitated taking it.

"If you don't want it I'll keep it," she said.

I took the Shivalinga.

****

Every morning I do the Hanuman Chalissa. No one knew I did this. One Thursday, Baba manifested a Hanuman pendant for me from a flower.

"This is for you," He said. Baba knows what we do.

I wore that pendant around my neck every day. The gold color began to change and a stone came out.

Shree and I were having a bite to eat before we left the house so I began to tease her.

"How can I wear the pendant like this? Why doesn't Baba give good-quality? Tell Baba to give good quality. I want to wear this."

We left directly after we finished eating. As Shree drove on the highway she touched Baba's photograph that hangs from the mirror.

"Take this. You asked for good-quality. There is a gold stamp on this one."

It was a Shirdi Baba pendant with a gold stamp on the back, validating it was pure gold.

****

Shree received a phone call from Srinivas Sanigepalli. His mother was in the hospital because of a heart attack. Before the phone call Shree was normal. After the phone call she went and lay down in her mom's bed. Suddenly Shree became very sick. I watched her face completely change. It changed so much I took a picture of her and sent it to Srinivas. He confirmed how much Shree's face looked like his mom as she lay in the hospital. His mom got better after Shree took on her sickness.

****

In May 2013 we visited Canada. Suddenly blood came from Shree's mouth and she was blind!

"I can't see," she told us.

She could not see or talk for about an hour. We were very scared.

That's when Baba came. He took His hand and held it over His eyes, and then He made a motion as if He was throwing the energy. Baba left. Shree could see again. Whose illness was it? We did not know.

****

One thing that is truly amazing to consider. When these bouts of sickness come on Shree she's never scared. At that time she is thinking about others. She never seems to think, *If I pray to Baba this will happen to me.* She simply does it because someone is in need.

GWYN MCGEE

Ashu (Asish Chandra) and I developed a mutual friendship by seeing each other at bhajans on Thursdays. Sometimes we texted words of encouragement during the week. We always promised that we would do lunch but it never happened.

In 2011 Shree, some family members, and a few devotees went on a trip to India. There was a small, dedicated group who continued to attend bhajans every Thursday.

One day I received a phone call from Ashu. He asked me if he could come by my home. I was pleasantly surprised and quickly replied yes. I felt honored that Ashu, a person who showed so much love and worked so well with Baba, wanted to visit my home.

We agreed on 3:30 p.m. as the designated time. When Ashu arrived and came inside he immediately mentioned he felt a peaceful energy, "If you become quiet enough you can hear the footsteps of God in here." It warmed my heart to hear Ashu's words.

He also told me Baba told him to come to my house. I was very surprised by that, but more surprised when Ashu said,

"Sometimes I can hear my sister Shree in Shirdi."

What did I think? I simply accepted his words. I had seen so much with Baba and I felt I knew Ashu's heart.

I asked Ashu if he wanted to see my altar.

"Yes," he replied, and he followed me down the stairs to my prayer space which was perhaps 5' x 6'.

Ashu and I sat side-by-side in front of my altar. He asked me questions about several objects before he focused on a small statue of Shirdi Sai Baba.

"What country did that statue come from?"

"I don't know," I replied.

"Did it come from India?"

"I don't know if it came from India," I said. "It was a gift from Bharosha Ma 's son-in-law."

After that we sat and talked with much love about Baba, the mandir and Shree. It was wonderful. We talked, perhaps, ten or fifteen minutes.

"Do you want to hear the aarti as it is played in Shirdi?" Ashu asked.

"Yes," I said.

He took out his cell phone and he began to play the aarti.

"Look. Here's a picture of Baba." An image of Shirdi Sai Baba appeared.

We listened to the aarti and enjoyed Baba's photo before Ashu suddenly said, "I can hear my sister, Shree. She sends you lots of love from Shirdi. Lots of love."

I was so pleased to receive such a message, any message about love. I accepted it wholeheartedly.

Next Ashu said, "She wants to give you something from Shirdi."

As he spoke his eyes opened and closed a bit as if he was somewhat in meditation. I sat no more than a foot away and waited for him to say something like Shree was going to bring me a souvenir. I never questioned if he was hearing Shree or not. I simply allowed the moment. The truth is I knew anything was possible with Baba and I trusted Ashu.

No more than ten seconds passed as I waited for Ashu to speak. Suddenly, he raised his hand very quickly and made a motion like someone would if they were catching a fly in-flight. Ashu turned his closed fist over and opened his hand. To my utter shock there was a pendant inside! It was a golden color with what looked like diamonds or rhinestones around an old image of Shirdi Sai Baba.

He passed it to me right away. I looked at the pendant; I looked at Ashu. I looked at the pendant again, placed it against my forehead, placed it against my heart and I put it on my altar.

Once again I was totally amazed! There was vibhuti…lots of vibhuti on the Shirdi Sai Baba statue that Ashu and I had discussed earlier.

We exchanged a few more words that had nothing to do with the miracle that just occurred. It was as if we didn't know how to acknowledge it.

Next Ashu said, "May I see it?" Referring to the pendant. "She told me to give it to you so quickly."

"Please," I said. I picked up the pendant and I handed it to Ashu.

I watched him look at it, kiss it, and give it back to me.

I replaced it on my altar.

Ashu and I continued to talk until my previous journalist brain finally screamed, Enough!

"Ashu! Wait a minute!" I said. "Has this ever happened to you before?"

His eyes became very wide and most innocent before he

said, "Not without my sister!"

I continued to question him. "Tell me what was going on when you were sitting with your eyes close."

"I could see my sister. She was in Shirdi. She told me that she sends you lots of love from Shirdi. Then she said she wanted to give you something from Shirdi and I knew she wanted me to give it to you. I asked her how was I supposed to do that. She said I am going to throw it to you. "Believe in me, Ashu."

I was stunned to hear, and truly accept that I saw Ashu catch the pendant that Shree Sai Baba threw from Shirdi India to my home in Brisbane, California. I saw proof of no time and space happen right before my eyes!

Moments later Ashu and I continued to talk before he interrupted our conversation. "Are you sure that vibhuti wasn't here before I got here?" He pointed to the very fresh vibhuti on the Shirdi Sai Baba murti.

"No, it was not here," I said, then laughed at the complexity of Baba's leelas.

Shree returned from Shirdi and for the first time visited my home with her mom, Don Olds and several family members. This was several weeks after the space and time miracle occurred. She took only a few steps into my house before Shree Sai Baba said, "I have been here before." She pointed around and down the stairs to my altar. When she saw my altar that day, and the vibhuti that was there, Shree acknowledged it was authentic.

****

I moved away from the San Francisco valley in December 2011. To keep in touch with Shree I developed a habit of texting endearments ever so often and she would reply with the same. Ashu and I also kept in contact that way.

In August of 2012 I began to experience some extreme abdominal discomfort. I noticed during that time Shree stop answering my texts. I asked Ashu to pray for me when he assisted Baba on Thursdays. After several weeks of pain one day it became unbearable and I lay down on my puja room floor.

"Baba," I said, "I love you. If you are going to kill me just kill me. I cannot take this, and I am not going to the hospital. I want to see you in South San Francisco first. You are the physician's physician."

A few minutes later as I lie on my stomach I felt a presence at my feet. Swiftly I looked to see who was there. I saw no one. When I laid down again this extremely cool air came in through my feet and worked it's way through my body into my head and out.

I spoke to Rameshji and Bharosha Ma that day, something I do once a month. She told me to call her for seven days of healing. On the 7th day Ashu texted me. He informed me Shree had surgery on her abdomen. It was a Friday.

Immediately the "coincidence" factor struck me that Shree was having surgery on her abdomen and I had been experiencing extreme abdominal discomfort. I texted Ashu about my observation.

"I find it interesting that Shree is having surgery on her abdomen at this time when I am experiencing abdominal problems. "

His simple reply was, "Yes, sister," and he did not comment further.

My symptoms lessened until they eventually disappeared. I continued to text Shree but heard nothing from her. By the beginning of September I made my first return trip to California. My first evening in the Bay Area I went to see Shree. She had experienced what she called the most serious surgery of this physical life. It involved forty-four stitches and a massive scar. During my days in South San Francisco, the majority of the nights I stayed with Anita and Naveen Goswami, but a few of those nights I stayed at Shree's. That is when she told me the surgery was mine, Ashu knew and that I would not have survived it.

"Did you notice I stopped texting you?"

"Yes."

"I knew it was yours and I just couldn't be in touch with you at such a time."

All the time on a deeper level I knew that was what had taken place, but to hear her say it was a whole other experience. I watched as she weathered lots of pain but still managed humor when I mentioned a scheduled doctors appointment.

Once I helped her as she struggled in the middle of the night. She said her recovery would take up to six months. I thanked her deeply and she told me to cherish times like the one we shared because they would not come again.

This was the second time I knew of, that Shree's body had taken on a major illness of mine.

In 2010, my blood pressure went so high I had dreams of death and knew something was terribly wrong.

Baba came after a bhajan and told me in front of an intimate crowd of maybe ten devotees, "You died, young lady. You need to thank my daughter. Do you know how difficult it is to give a new life?"

I was shocked to the bone. I mumbled something about my dreams with death symbologies. In one of the dreams I heard Baba's voice. It was accompanied by a symbol acknowledging my life had been extended.

"You will help Anita write," Baba said. "You will help her explain the past." Later, when He gave darshan through Shree He told me, "You stroked out. You had eight strokes. You are maya. You are not here."

That was the first time Shree Sai Baba took my karma of health problems onto Her body. It was directly after that Anita Bawa and I began to write Shree Shirdi Sai Baba of South San Francisco: Divine Touch.

In 2012, while I visited Shree during her recovery from my surgery, twice she mentioned how Baba said I would write a second book, a collection of devotee's experiences. She urged me to return in three weeks to attend Shirdi Sai Baba's birthday celebration. Shree said I should thank Him directly for taking on my illness. I wanted to but I was uncertain about returning so quickly, leaving my husband again. Eventually I felt a quick return to South San Francisco was extremely important, and when I shared my decision with Larry, as usual, he was supportive.

At Baba's birthday celebration I thanked Him during darshan.

"For what?" He said and answered the question with a question. "For taking your pain?"

"Yes," I replied.

"And now you are worried about her."

As I nodded 'yes' He began to edge His way to the end of His chair. Before I knew it Baba was standing before me, and He sat down and got up three times in rapid succession.

"She will be fine," He assured.

With that startling revelation, knowing Shree had barely been able to walk over the last few days, I said to Baba. "Your daughter tells me there will be a second book."

"Yes, write a second book. And ask them all for their experiences." He pointed toward the crowd and swept His arm from one side of the room to the other.

That is how Baba told me to write Devotees Speak.

After bhajans I shared Baba's request for a second book with the crowd. A few days later I returned to Smyrna, Georgia. I did what I could to get the book underway by requesting written submissions, but with the passage of time I realized interviewing devotees would be a more fruitful method for gathering material.

I attended an Akhanda Bhajans…World Peace bhajans in Georgia that November, and received a beautiful laminated presentation of Sathya Sai Baba's 'Prayer of Surrender' from the hosts, RJ and Asha Patel. I felt inclined to read it every day for several weeks.

Approximately five months later I scheduled another trip to California to attend Shivaratri, visit friends, and collect experiences for Shree Sai Baba of South San Francisco: Devotees Speak. About one month before my March 10, 2013 flight, I began to experience a milder version of what I had experienced approximately nine months before, and once again Shree stopped texting me. This time I knew it was not a coincidence. About a week before I flew to South San Francisco I heard Shree was spitting up blood again; something she has done through the years when she had taken on someone's cancer. I was concerned for her, and inside wondered if it were mine… but it is not easy to consider such a situation.

The first night I slept in South San Francisco at Anita's home I had a dream. Baba came in the form of Shree, held me in His arms, and told me I had cancer. After He told me, in the dream, I felt a deep sense of realization about my condition, then I acknowledged the truth of it, and finally I felt the deepest sense of peace as His arms continued to enfold me. Immediately after I felt those feelings, they slowly faded out of my body into Baba's body. I could see that energy leaving my body and going into His. It was so beautiful and compassionate how Baba came and told me I had cancer. Part of Baba's Surrender Prayer that I read daily for weeks is:

"Do you want me to deal with it...yes or no? Then you must stop being anxious about it! I shall guide you only if you completely surrender to Me, and when I must lead you into a different path than the one you expect, I carry you in My arms."

Baba literally carried me in His arms in that dream.

Baba gave darshan the Thursday before the Shivaratri celebration was scheduled, and I told myself I would not ask Him about my sickness. When I went before Him He asked me about the book. I told Him I had interviewed several devotees and many more would be participating, although I knew He already knew.

"I AM happy," He said, and He manifested a rudraksha for me.

Although I had told myself I would not ask about my illness, being human I could not resist.

"Baba, what about this body?"

"What about this body?" He replied.

"I have been experiencing some digestive issues lately....."

He tilted His head to the left and just looked into my eyes with love and patience. His entire expression said, I have told you your condition and I am taking care of it... but He never said a word.

With that I threw up both my hands, "That's okay, Baba."

I had received the message loud and clear and there was no need for words.

"Will the book be ready by your birthday next year?" I asked

119

knowing His answer would reveal how much of an ordeal I would endure in the coming months.

There was the very slightest of hesitations before He replied, "Yes," and He touched my face and said. "I love you. I AM happy."

After bhajans that evening, Shree fell on the stairs, and it took nearly twenty minutes to revive Her. At one point I rubbed one of Her feet as her mother requested. She wanted to keep Shree's feet and hands warm. It was only when I was on my way to Anita's house that I realized my hands were saturated with the most powerful perfumed smell of jasmine.

From that night on I dreamed nearly every night. Two sources connected with South San Francisco informed me that Baba would not be giving darshan for two to three months because Shree had taken on someone's cancer. I cried for Her thinking that it may be mine...and I prayed for Shree, knowing in a sense I was praying for God.

The dreams continued to come, some involved blood. In one dream there was blood on some bed pillows and sheets, I knew they were Shree's, where she had been coughing up blood as she lie in bed. Still, overall I had dreams of God's Grace and loving support.

I finally saw a doctor and that led to a CT scan. The CT scan revealed my liver was an area of concern and that led to an MRI. They also scheduled a colonoscopy. The colonoscopy concerned me the most because of the pain I had experienced, and because two prior physicians concluded, after physical exams, there was something in my colon that was of concern.

Yet when all the tests results were in nothing of consequence was found anywhere.

During my July, 2013 visit to South San Francisco Shree Sai Baba confirmed my cancer dream revealed the truth.

ANTONIO MOYA

Note: **Before I spoke to Antonio, Juan Arias contributed the foundation of Antonio's experience.**

This experience is more notorious because Antonio Moya, a member of my family who authorized me to share it on his behalf, is a skeptic when it comes to religious, devotional...pious things. I think this makes this experience different because it is harder for a person who isn't familiar with these kinds of things to accept.

In October, 2012, Miriam Gomez, who is Antonio's friend, invited him to go to South San Francisco to see this lady. They were going to go on a Thursday.

Antonio is the kind of person that is always doing service for others, helping people; helping Miriam with her brother, Livio, who had two strokes and is now handicapped. He helps take them places when needed, and the reason he was going to South San Francisco was to help take them there. Antonio thought he would not be able to go because it was impossible for him to get off of work during the week.

"No-no," he said, "Don't count on me."

But during that particular time Antonio had very serious problems about steady work...work that paid well and some other issues, and he was at the end of his rope with work and money problems. He told me just that. Because of the unstable nature of his job Antonio was considering going to see the South San Francisco lady anyway. I told him to ask Shirdi Baba for help. I told him to ask because I know Shirdi Baba. I have been to India. For a person like Antonio who is not into this kind of thing it is difficult to do, but he decided to go and ask. This was a difficult decision for him, because Antonio was disconnected from spiritual things. He didn't believe in that.

When Antonio was in South San Francisco Baba came in the way that He does to that lady, and Antonio saw him there. He returned to his apartment and something happened.

He said to me, "Isn't this strange? I was lying in my bed the next morning and I heard a voice. It was speaking Spanish and it was very clear.

It said, 'Don't worry. You will be okay. You are going to have peace. You are going to rest.'"

Antonio was a little...he thought...maybe I'm going to die. Where is this voice coming from?

"It sounded.... It's kind of strange but.... I don't know how Baba of Shirdi sounds but this was a female voice, and I believe it was Shirdi Baba's voice because I had just come from seeing Him."

He went on to tell me, "But I don't have a car. I don't have a means for getting from here to there. I'm really down."

Right after this happened they called him to work but that job was not fine for him. He didn't have a car.... He couldn't get a car because he didn't have a job....

Within two months time Antonio went back to see the

Shirdi lady. While he was there She gave him a Lakshmi pendant. I said to him this must mean something. Lakshmi stands for prosperity. Abundance. And so Antonio kept the pendant in his pocket but still he worried.

Then he received the phone call. This company gave him work and gave him a car.

Later Antonio said, " That voice.... I was not sleeping. I was not dreaming. I still hear that voice. After that these things came one after the other. Good things."

Since then Antonio goes to the devotional centers to say, "Thank you".

SUNEEL MUKKAM

I came to know about the Baba mandir in South San Francisco about two years ago (2011) through a friend, Srinivas Sanigepalli, who is a regular attendee. He invited me to come on a Thursday and my first visit was a totally different experience from the other temples I go to. Normally I pray by myself or with my family. This was totally new for me. My first visit felt different from my second visit with a group. That feeling changed when I focused on the bhajans. During my second visit Baba came. All of my life I have gone to temple and prayed and nothing. After temple I would go home, but this.... That first time when Baba came I didn't know any protocol. I went up and touched His feet. They gave me this white piece of paper and I saw a flower in Baba's hand.

"Do you have any questions?" Baba asked.

"No. Just bless me Baba."

I didn't ask Baba anything. I just closed my eyes and when I looked again I saw a flower and a ring on the paper. It was an amazing feeling. I don't know how to express it. Shirdi Sai Baba was on the ring. After that I received two mandalas...pendants, all Shirdi Baba.

****

The most touching story of my life happened in 2011. I fell very sick on May 18th and was hospitalized in Kaiser Permanente Hospital in San Francisco. I was in the hospital for several days when Srinivas Sanigepalli and Narendra Kothakota came to see me. They told me on the previous Thursday, before bhajans at the South San Francisco temple, Naren told my sister, Shree, how I had gotten sick all of a sudden and was in the hospital. They showed my picture to the devotees who were there and they prayed for my well-being and quick recovery. I was in the hospital for a week. After I returned home Shree called me on the telephone.

"You will be recovering very soon. We prayed a couple of times for you."

I went to the mandir in July and had Baba's darshan. I touched Baba's feet and once again I didn't ask Baba anything.

"You will recover, fully, and it will not happen to you again. You will recover 100%."

With so-o many devotees He knew Suneel. He knew what suffering I was going through.

My recovery was faster than expected. Three experts; a neurology specialist, a general physician and a chiropractor were surprised by my progress. They said it would take at least six months. I recovered, fully, and returned to work in August, which also surprised my work colleagues.

This was a life-changing event for me. On the one hand all the doctors said it would take a minimum of six month for me to recover and that I would never recover back to normal. Three months down the road I could see I had fully recovered, and that reminded me of all of Baba's blessings.

"You will fully recover. It will not happen to you again."

Whenever I am afraid the same thing will happen to me, I find belief and strength in Baba's words.

MAMTA NANDA

I started going to the South San Francisco mandir in 2003. In 2004 I woke up with a slight headache that progressed throughout the day to a splitting headache that no medication would alleviate. I decided I needed to go to the ER and my husband took me.

During my examination they gave me a CT scan and some painkillers. I felt somewhat better but not totally, and both my eyes were very red. They gave me another dose of medication.

The doctors saw a gray area in my brain during the CT scan and determined I needed to go for an MRI. They said it should be done immediately. I thought, *Oh my God, Baba!*

I finally went for the MRI. I was very scared. I actually held onto a locket that Baba manifested for me. I could feel it pulling in my hand. You are not supposed to have anything metal with you during an MRI but I told them, "I am sorry. I am going to hold this locket."

I received a phone call a couple of days later. The doctor said I needed a second MRI because they saw something; a small growth on my pituitary gland. I was so scared. Thursday came and I went to puja. I told Baba that I was very worried. I told Him the endocrinologist wanted to do a second MRI to see if the small tumor was benign.

"Don't worry," He said.

He removed a flower from one of the malas that people bring. He rubbed that flower all over my head, all over my back, on the two sides of my neck and He said, "You will be fine. I am with you and you will be fine."

Normally when He does that, when He rubs the flower over any part of your body something is not right. He is taking the pain. He is removing the pain so I knew something was not right.

I went back for the second MRI.

"There was a tumor there but now we cannot see it. I don't know why we cannot see it. It seems like it would have been a benign one." That's what the endocrinologist said. She was very surprised.

In the back of my mind I was thinking, *Oh my God!* I had tears and goosebumps and I was very thankful to Baba that He had helped me that way. Because basically, with Baba's blessings the tumor disappeared.

****

I was packing for a trip to Malaysia in 2009 and I couldn't find my wedding ring. I prayed to Baba. *Where is it?* There was this one place that I looked over and over again. I really searched that place and my ring wasn't there.

I texted Shree about my wedding ring. Fifteen minutes after I texted her she replied back. She told me to look in that particular place. I looked and the ring was right there! It was a place that I looked so many times; I moved things around; I checked it thoroughly, and now my ring was there.

****

After going through the MRI I developed claustrophobia. I felt very trapped in closed-in places. I'm from Malaysia. I have to travel back on a plane, and it's a long plane ride. From 2008 to 2009 my claustrophobia increased. I couldn't go anywhere. I felt like the windows were closing in on me. I felt suffocated. I would develop an anxiety attack and begin to sweat. I felt so bad. Going to Malaysia was one of my biggest issues. How was I going to do this? I went to Cincinnati, that was a short trip and I was a wreck. I chanted Baba's name throughout the flight and I felt better. But Malaysia would be a much longer flight. I didn't know what I was going to do. I had gotten to a point where even in the shopping malls I needed to know where the exits were. In hotels, whatever. Only chanting Baba's name helped me.

I went to Baba and I told Him about it. I was in tears.

In the end I said, "I feel stupid saying this but this is how I feel."

"I am with you. Don't be afraid," was all He said.

The moment He said that there was a big change. I felt something just lifting. I felt really light. I felt....'Ooooo I'm going to fly now'. I felt this energy just swoop out of me. It was an indescribable feeling.

My trip to Malaysia came and I attended bhajans right before my flight. I ran up during darshan and got Baba's blessings.

He said, "Remember, I will be there with you on the plane. Don't worry."

Well…I even surprised myself. I was fantastic. If I felt a little tingling I would chant Baba's name and I was fine. Even to this day I don't really think about the windows, etc. If I experience any fear, be it a small amount of claustrophobia or issues in my family life or my marriage, I simply think about Shree and Baba, and I speak to them. Immediately I feel relief.

****

After two girls, I really wanted a son. We attempted to get pregnant for at least a year with no luck. We went to the doctor and he told us to try all kinds of things, and we were doing what we could naturally.

During a particular bhajan Baba called out to the group, "Who wants a baby?"

"Me," I said.

"You want a child?" He questioned.

"Yes I do," and I told Baba we had been trying.

Immediately He said, "Before October you will be pregnant."

"Really Baba? Are you sure?" I replied.

He just smiled at me.

"Okay Baba," I said to Him. "I have full faith in You."

October was approaching. We were trying and I said to my husband, "I have full faith in Baba. It will happen."

It was at the end of September 2008 and I was in Target. I was just shopping. I thought, *Okay. I'm going to get a pregnancy test and try it out.*

I went to the restroom and tried the test. It was positive. *Oh my God.* I called Shree and my husband from the bathroom. I told them I was pregnant.

"I told you so-o," Shree replied.

It was right on the dot. The next day was October 1st.

That Thursday I went to bhajans and Baba asked me one thing. "Are you happy?"

"Yes, Baba I am happy."

Of course, I love my girls, but in an Indian family you always want at least one boy. So to top it off as I went back to my seat, Baba said, "It is going to be a boy."

I was totally blissed.

I didn't go for the scan where you can find out the sex of the child. My husband questioned, "How can you be so sure?"

I said, "I have full faith in my Baba. And now we have two girls and a boy.

****

Sometimes Shree does not want to tell you something is wrong. She will give you messages along the way. Lots of time she's said things that later on I said, "Oh my God. That's what she was saying." My experience has been whatever Shree says will happen.

****

In Malaysia there is a place where my mom and I go that is like a temple. A Sufi saint is there. He spoke to me and told me I needed to do a special puja, prayer, in my house. He said I would find the right person. I knew someone special needed to perform the ceremony for me, but in the US I didn't know anyone who would. He assured me I would find someone. I thought of how Baba, Shirdi Baba, was considered a kind of saint, and that perhaps because of His history that He would be able to perform the ceremony.

I told my mom about what I was thinking and she took

what I was thinking to the Sufi gentlemen. My mom told him a little bit about Shree. She said he kept quiet then went into a kind of trance.

He opened his eyes, "Of course. That is the person I was talking about."

My mom left the house, and as she approached the gate she realized the gentleman had run out behind her. We had never seen that man get up and leave where he normally sits. When he reached my mom he said, "Your daughter is very lucky that this person will be doing the puja. The chosen one. She is very high, very high in the spiritual hierarchy."

SHREE SAI BABA

ANANDARAM NUGGIHALLI

I'm a regular guy who has been doing spiritual practices for many years. I've always been interested in spirituality. The first time I walked into the South San Francisco mandir during bhajans it felt like "Holy Moley, what is going on here?" I had been to Sai bhajans before and they were always nice but this was so...wow. I felt like...what have we been missing? The vibratonal level of the bhajans was high even though they were a bit loud. My mind swarmed. I'd heard about Shree and there was the expectation that Baba might come and the spookiness of that. I thought, *Is anything going to happen here? You know... that thing?* It was like some kind of circus, and all the people were expecting a performance. My take on bhajans was about feeling the vibrations in your heart and opening up to God, so I was sort of uneasy with what I felt there. I sensed the desires of the people around me, and I sat there sort of praying, *Baba, don't come like that. I hope nothing happens.* And guess what? Nothing happened! He didn't come that day and I was very relieved. Later we met Shree and she was amazing.

We returned to the mandir two weeks later; my mom wanted

to go. My sister, Malani, (Keshavaprasad) went with us. This time Baba came. I watched it all, and maybe fifteen minutes later as I sat there I gazed a bit to the right of Baba as He sat in His chair. All of a sudden I could see the totality of me! My ego...my entire self in a way I had never experienced. It was as if for one second on a TV screen I got to see the whole thing. No qualifications. No sadhana. No do a lot of seva before I give you anything. Just like that! The ultimate was given to me about myself; all that was left was to truly get to know Him.

When I went up for darshan He placed a garland around my neck. I knew it was related to what I had experienced. My mom felt it also had to do with my dad passing away, that it was Baba's special way of honoring my new position in my family. Until this day Baba has never placed a garland around my neck again.

****

In the beginning when I went to the South San Francisco mandir I still had doubts.

I thought...*they say this is Shirdi Baba but how do I know?* Questions like, 'Is He (Shirdi Baba who comes through Shree) legit?' And if He is legit so what? I didn't really know who Shirdi Baba was. Everybody who was into Shirdi Baba worshipped Him as God. I also pondered the possibility that maybe it was some other spirit getting into her body and we all thought it was Shirdi Baba. I didn't want to be caught by some body or some thing.... I was reading books about Edgar Cayce at the time and I didn't want to be used by some random spirit who was pretending to be someone that I wanted to be present in the mandir. The truth is I was scared.

But something happened. As I continued to attend bhajans

I began to realize how deeply connected I was with Sathya Sai Baba. My knowledge of Sathya Sai Baba came from my childhood. My parents believed in Sathya Sai Baba but for me that was as far as it went. For a period of time I also had doubts about Sathya Sai Baba. I never knew I had a connection with Him until I started attending the South San Francisco mandir, and as I attended my fears and my doubts around God began to dissolve. A trust grew and a relationship developed. We would go to Shree's house outside of bhajans and religious celebrations and Baba would come. He became my one-on-one teacher. Sometimes He taught through feelings and a profound silence. I came to know what I meant to Baba and that there was no separation between us.

****

Shree and Maya.... I experienced Maya as a master teacher during a stretch of time when Shree was extremely ill and the pain she experienced was intolerable. Shree could not stay in her body so Maya took her place. One simple yet powerful teaching Maya shared with me at a time when I was dealing with what would have resulted in an extremely high dollar business deal: "The fruit of greed is bad."

****

I never got to see Sathya Sai Baba produce a lingam from His mouth. We were told if you saw that event this would be your last birth.

A few years ago I was having a tough time. I didn't want to continue with life because of misgivings and other things. Life seemed like a burden. During that time Shree went to Sacramento and she invited us to go. My wife, Geetha, went but I didn't. While she was there Shree produced a Lakshmi from her mouth. Once again I missed it! Later I told Shree I was fed up but she already knew how badly I was feeling. Within a week's time, during the next bhajans, Baba cleared me of those strong feelings. Just cleared it out. Within days I told Ashu (Asish Chandra) "As long as Baba Himself can come here; I can come here to serve Him." I went from wanting to be history to that state of mind.

****

While the world was discovering how ill Sathya Sai Baba was in India Shree had surgery. Geetha and I went to her home to help in whatever way we could. The doctor advised that she not straighten her back until a certain amount of healing took place.

Shree was keenly aware of what was happening in Puttaparthi.

"Check the news," she said, but then she would tell us the details before we heard them on the news.

On the very last night before Sathya Sai Baba passed away Geetha and I were there along with some members of Shree's family. Several times Shree said, "Find out what is the latest news from Puttaparthi."

Inder (Pandher) got on the internet and reported what was occurring with Sathya Sai Baba.

"Check me for those conditions," Shree instructed.

Each time they were the same as Sathya Sai Baba's. They were the same. I thought, *What is going on here?*

Geetha and I remained in Shree's room and I was directing healing energy toward her. Shree got up from the bed and began to walk with her hands behind her back. Her hair was fluffed out all over her head, although Shree's hair is totally straight.

I watched her walk, wearing this floor length house gown, and I said very naivelly, "Shree, you're walking just like Sathya Sai Baba."

He turned, looked at me and said, "Do you want to see Me run?"

Immediately I said, "No-no-no. Your stitches will come out."

"If I-I run nothing will happen," He replied before He entered the bathroom.

This 'watch' of what was happening in India and what was taking place with Shree went on until around one in the morning. Eventually Shree went to sleep.

Around eleven o'clock the next morning Geetha and Nani (Parvati Lal) were downstairs preparing food for a party that was going to be held at Justin's (Lal) house. Inder and I were upstairs with Shree. Once again Shree got up and began to walk like Sathya Sai Baba. Her straight hair was totally fluffed up all around her head and her hands were behind her back. This time Baba went into the mandir.

"Go and call Nani," He said.

Quickly I did as I was told. Both Geetha and Nani rushed up the stairs.

"Baba is here," I told Nani as I stood near the staircase.

Nani walked straight over to a large photo of Sathya Sai Baba that hung on the wall. She stared at that photo.

"No, Nani. He's right here," I told her.

Nani turned and she saw that Sathya Sai Baba was in her daughter.

As Nani stood in front of that photo of Sathya Sai Baba,

Baba walked pass Nani toward the entrance of Shree's bedroom. As He passed Nani He looked at her. He looked at Nani in the exact fashion that Sathya Sai Baba in Puttaparthi looked at someone during darshan. Because of that direct darshan Nani was in tears.

He turned around and looked at Geetha. "Did you get enough?" He asked.

After that Baba walked back into Shree's bedroom and was about to go into the bathroom....

It seemed He would go into the bathroom and Shree would come out sometimes or Baba would come back...you never knew what was going on. Typically, He would go into the bathroom and disappear, but that last time before Sathya Sai Baba entered the bathroom He said, "That's it! I'm all done."

From the sounds that came out of the bathroom I assumed Shree was taking a shower. When she emerged from the bathroom she wore a white dress and she went and lie down on the bed. I noticed her face looked dark.

"Your face looks dark, Shree," I told her. "It actually looks blue."

"Code Blue," she said.

That was around one o'clock. After that we went home.

While we were at her house Shree invited us to Justin's party, but we decided not to go because of the hours we had already spent away from home. When she called us and invited us again we went.

It was a regular party, and the majority of the young people there were not interested in Sai Baba. We were sitting with Shree when we saw the media was reporting Sathya Sai Baba passed away. As the party unfolded around us the story of Baba's passing unfolded on television, and somehow in the background of this party I heard a bhajan playing. This woman was singing,

"Sri Lakshmi Ramana, Narayana. Om Anantha Narayana". Anantha...The Eternal One.... Right then something hit me in my heart and I began to sob in the midst of the party. In my life I had basically two darshans that I recall of Sathya Sai Baba in India, and now I was literally sobbing for everybody to see.

Shree sat above me on the couch and I sat on the floor to her left.

"Bhaiya," she said and placed her hand on my shoulder. Then a few moments later she said, "If you cry like this when He leaves what will you do when I leave?"

I pulled myself together a bit and I went and sat in another chair. Another fifteen minutes passed and everyone was doing whatever they were doing, and again tears came to my eyes out of nowhere.

Shree looked at me "What? Still crying?" Then HE said, " I'm right here".

I went straight to Baba and hugged Him.

Note: Geetha Nuggenhalli, who was present as her husband Anand shared this experience, contributed the statement where Baba said to her, "Did you get enough?". She also stated it was confirmed the time that Shree said, "Code Blue," was the exact time they were attempting to resuscitate Sathya Sai Baba in the Super Specialty Hospital.

****

There are times when Baba comes outside of bhajans, and this particular time several of us were present. Two of us heard Him speaking and were quite aware that He was speaking, another person appeared to have heard Him speaking but later spoke as if what He said was totally erased from their memory, and a fourth person, physically present, never heard Him speak at all.

****

I have seen physical evidence of the comings and goings of Maya. Once during a social gathering Maya got up to go to the bathroom. She was slender; her stomach completely flat. When she emerged from the bathroom she spoke to us as if she had not seen us for a long time. I realized it was Shree. Her stomach was much bigger; not flat at all. No one can manipulate their body on cue to that degree. Later Maya got up and danced the twist. Trim. Fit. So much dancing. When she sat down, Shree returned. Shree was sweating profusely and her stomach appeared to be the size of a woman's stomach who was around six months pregnant.

Maya affected men and women in many ways. She was a force to be reckoned with. Ultimately after quite a struggle I was blessed to experience Her energy as that of the Divine Mother.

****

A group of us, devotees, slept in the mandir one night during the early part of 2011. During another sleep over occasion when Baba came I said, "It's like Shirdi."

"It is," He confirmed.

The next day after the sleepover in 2011 Baba came again. He looked at the photograph in which He is leaning against a wall and an umbrella is being held over His head.

"That photo was taken on the last day. I was feeling very sick. I didn't want to walk but my devotees asked me to. I made one last walk around the village to give darshan. On that day I took samadhi."

I've always had this weird curiosity about what it feels like to be walled up like the body is walled up for samadhi, so that day I asked Baba, "What is it like to be inside the samadhi?" Now I think what a dumb question.

But then He looked at me and said, "Silly question." Then He said, "I took samadhi in the Hearts of my devotees."

****

Baba told us that He was going to take care of the Deep Horizon oil spill in the Gulf of Mexico. Not long after He said that it was reported that a naturally forming oil eating bacteria had taken care of the spill.

After I totally accepted who Baba was, and that He was the One who was coming into Shree, I asked Him this question during one of His impromptu question and answer sessions, "Like this world, how many worlds do you manage?"

"Can it be counted?" He replied. His answer was so full of patience. It blew me away.

****

One of Shree's spiritual brother's in Sacramento. California, Iqbal, was in a coma in the hospital. He was very kind to Shree when her car wrecked and he gave her one of his cars. That is the kind of heart that he had. Geetha and I were in the room with Shree when his wife called and told Shree he was in really bad shape, and she did not know if he would make it through. They got off the telephone and Shree said let's pray for him. We prayed in silence for maybe five minutes. Shree was the first to speak.

"I think he's fine now."

A phone call came. Iqbal himself was calling. The man who was in a coma was on the telephone. When I met him in person a couple of months later...there was a light in his eyes. He had experienced something that could never be taken away from him.

GEETHA NUGGIHALLI

My in-laws and my parents were into Sai Baba but I was not. My sister-in-law, Malani, and her husband, Keshava lived in Puttaparthi but they traveled to the states quite often. They began to tell us about the South San Franciso mandir and encouraged us to go. Malani said we should go see who she called "Trance Baba". From her exuberant descriptions it sounded more like a show of miracles than a spiritual event. I was into spirituality and I really wasn't interested in seeing a show. I did not want to go. Keshava was in town in 2006, and through a set of circumstances he asked us to give him a lift so that he could visit with our family. We agreed and where did we end up? At the mandir.

I did not want to be there so I sat all the way in the back. The music was loud and.... I was very uncomfortable. I felt like I was at a freak show where the people were waiting for a performance. 'Trance Baba' as Malani called Him did not come, but there was a white robe that was placed near the end of bhajans on the large chair where Baba sits. I saw that robe puff up as if there was a body in it. The body was inside the robe.

I could see that as if His Presence was there. I have never seen that happen again until this day.

It may have been two weeks later when I ended up at the mandir, and once again I sat in the back. When Baba came into Shree, I said in my mind, *You are such a beautiful soul. Why do you want to do this?* I got an answer.

"I do this so I can get the people to connect to me. To raise them up."

After I heard that answer within me...something shifted in me.

We had no intention of returning to the mandir, but there we were two weeks later. At the time I was not still fully connected to what was unfolding there, but Baba came into Shree and He called us up. He placed a garland on Anand, and when He called me forward...I have no idea what He said to me...I have no idea what He did to me, but tears poured down my face. My heart opened. I don't normally show my emotions so much but even after I returned to my seat I was still crying.

"Why are you crying?" Malani, who sat next to me asked.

"There's so much love. So much love," I replied.

You don't experience that kind of love normally. It's so unconditional, so divine, so special. It pulled me in and opened me up. Now whenever He comes I cry. It is like a blossoming of me from inside.

During a later date when Anand was talking to Baba Anand said, "We came here because of Keshava".

Baba laughed. "Right. I made him bring you here, and now he is not here anymore and you are still coming."

****

The love that you receive is amazing. We started going to the mandir in August, 2006 and my youngest brother unexpectedly passed away in October from a massive heart attack. My parents, who were in their seventies, lived with him and they were totally devastated. He clutched his chest and passed away sitting beneath a photograph of Shirdi Sai Baba on October 15th...the day Shirdi Baba took samadhi. One woman remarked how his funeral was like no other. The energy was so high and positive. Baba gave me the strength during those fourteen days to talk about God and His miracles. I could never have done this before. When I saw Baba at darshan, once my parents were settled in our home in California, I said, "You prepared me for this."

Baba brought me to South San Francisco. There was no way I could have done all that I did involving my brother's passing. No way I could have handled it.

****

During the days when we first came to the mandir Shree fell down the stairs and injured either her ankle or leg very badly. She was limping and I could see she was in pain.

Baba came after bhajans one day.

"Does anyone have anything to ask?"

The room was basically quiet.

"No one wants to ask about your sister?" Baba said.

Everyone was silent.

"Don't you want her to be better?"

All of us answered, "Yes".

The majority of the crowd dispersed and there was a hand full of us who remained.

Baba came back and said, "Hmmm. Sooo. What do you all want?"

There were about ten of us, and we replied we wanted Him to take care of Shree.

"Okay," He said.

So He requested the wrap around His ankle be removed. While it was being removed He said things and made noises indicating there was a lot of pain, but after the bandage was gone Baba flexed His foot and Shree was healed. No more problem. It was done.

With Baba there is the flair and drama of the Krishna energy; Shiva giving you the diksha, and the Mother pouring out the love.

****

In 2011 Shree invited me to join a trip she was taking to India. I really wanted to go but with my kids being young it was very difficult. After Shree invited me again and because of how much I wanted to go at one point I said, "Do something, Baba!" Miraculously one of my relatives offered to come and take care of the kids, and I was able to take the trip.

We visited several places. People picked us up and hosted us. Finally we went to Shirdi. We landed, and were at the airport but there was no one to welcome us. My heart cried. I thought, *This is Shirdi. This is Your place. Your daughter is here and there is no one to welcome her.*

Some of the group approached cabs and asked if they could take us to a hotel, but I just stood there. Then suddenly, out of nowhere this man came up.

"So where are you from?" he asked.

We told him, and he started talking to us. He was a Shirdi Baba devotee. He began to talk to Shree, and at some point Shree asked us to give them a moment to speak alone. We stepped away a short distance. I could see his face but I couldn't see hers. As they talked I watched his face transform from shock to bliss...literally. And Shree's back changed. It became Baba's back. I know His back when I see it.

Afterwards the man walked over to us. "Don't go anywhere. I am going to organize everything."

He got a van and took us to a restaurant. I ate the best food I'd had the entire trip. After the meal he simply said, "Take care. The driver will take you where you need to go." We never saw that man again. It was a wonderful welcome.

We continued on and entered Shirdi.

I walked behind Shree as we climbed a set of stairs, and suddenly she said, "Bhabi," her voice somewhat strained. She sat down on the stairs like Baba sits, and her entire scalp was white with vibhuti.

I tried to lift her but I couldn't. I ran and got one of the men to help. We were able to take Her to the room.

Baba had come. There was so much vibhuti you could not see any black hair. There was so much vibhuti it was falling from Her head. The word spread and people came to visit Him. We began to dust the vibhuti from Her head and put it in packages. So many local people came. The young. The poor. They were amazed and so grateful for the live darshan of Baba. It made me realize this is so special. It should not be taken for granted.

We were in Shirdi for two or three days and Baba gave darshan throughout the time we were there. It got to the point where we had to tell visitors He is sleeping...He is resting... please give Him a break. There were swarms of people. When we went out to eat Shree would totally cover her head so no one could see the vibhuti.

I got to sit and watch Baba in action in Shirdi; the kindness

He gave to the little children. It was beautiful. The love flowed. It was very special.

****

I have seen Shree so sick.... You can't watch the suffering. I've gone up to Baba many times and asked, "Why? And asked if I could help by taking some of it.

His answers: a smile a gentle "No."

"This is what she has come here for."

"Your body can not take it. (referring to any normal body) Her body is special."

I have seen how special her body is. She has been so sick and minutes later she's just fine. We've gone to the hospital and they are doing a million things to her. Three hours later she's just fine. And the hospital can't find anything. They do all the tests and nothing.

****

I have been with Shree and she said, "There's a heart attack," and she experienced a pain in her chest. That's how she knew.

She has said, "There's an IV."

There, on her arm, I saw the skin puff up at the point where the IV was started.

What these experiences have brought out in me is the compassion, the caring, the love for someone else. She could hide the whole thing but the purpose was to evoke that part of me. If I can be that way with her I can be that way with others.

There have been times when Baba has come while Shree is sick.

"Don't do anything," He said, "I am actually doing psychic

surgery on her. Leave her alone and she will be okay."

Afterwards He would give a certain amount of time that the process will take.

I have seen Shree vomiting blood. It happens so often and is almost always related to someone who has cancer.

Baba has literally said when Shree is sick, suffering and tired, and He comes in as Maya who is strong and energetic, "This is Me. The sickness does not affect Me."

****

The teachings that pop in when Maya comes are very special. She is tough; she's to the point and she blessings you so much. There is huge growth with Maya. It can be difficult because she is a no nonsense Being.

****

One evening we were going to take a ride to Stockton.

Baba came. "I don't want you driving. There is a danger for you. Watch out because something will come up."

"Sure. No problem, Baba."

Normally, I don't drive. Anand drives.

Sure enough, that weekend my cousin invited me to a puja at her house.

I told her we couldn't come but she didn't understand.

I talked to Shree/Maya about it and she said, "I told you something would come up. If you must go, go. But don't you drive."

Still Anand decided we should not go. About a week passed and nothing happened. I was a little skeptical. I thought, *perhaps it's nothing.* We drove to bhajans the following Thursday

---

159

and a car came right into our lane on my side! Anand swerved just in time.

"Did you see that?!" Anand said.

It would have hit us for sure. That happened one week after Baba warned me of danger.

****

We decided we would chant the Hanuman Chalissa for twenty-four hours.

We chanted from midnight Monday to midnight Tuesday. A few of us were the core of the event. Shree, Nani. (Parvati Lal), Inder, Manav, Hardip Kaur, and Anand was in and out. There were others who came and went as well. But the core group participated the entire time. Shree, along with a few of us, was fasting one hundred percent. No eating or drinking. At one point Shree couldn't sit anymore and we got something and laid her on it. The next thing I knew she passed out. She lay there totally unconscious with her palm open and facing upwards. Time passed. Maybe thirty minutes, and there was no one near Shree; just a pillow under her head. In her open palm was a murti of Hanuman. There was no flower. Nothing. Simply the murti of Hanuman that appeared in her hand.

****

Around September 2012 Shree called me early one morning and asked me to come to her house. I didn't go right then, and I received another call.

"Come, right now! If you don't come right now you're not going to see it. It's going to start fading."

I jumped up and got my mom to come with me.

When we arrived Shree's face was the face of Hanuman. Her lower lip was very enlarged and very red. Her lip was the same color as the Hanuman's murti in the mandir.

****

My mom was in India in December, 2012 and some things weren't going too smoothly for her. During that time Baba gave darshan and He told me, "Go. Bring her here."

Shree was planning a trip to India. We decided that I would go with her and bring my mom back to the states afterwards.

The following Thursday Baba gave another darshan. I went before Him. "I've already told you to go get your mom."

"But can't I go when Shree goes?"

"No. If you wait you will not be able to bring her here."

I got scared. I took a flight to India the next week, which was in January, 2013, and I brought her back with me.

During a darshan with Baba in February He said, "Your mom would have had a very bad stroke. Had she been in India she would have lingered and passed on."

My mom had a few ups some downs after that. In May Baba spoke to me again about my mom.

"Her time has come. But don't worry. I will take care of it."

The very last day of May, 2013, in the middle of the night my mom went to the bathroom and fell and broke her shoulder. She did not call my dad or me. She dragged herself back to the bedroom and lie on the floor beside her bed. When my dad realized where she was he called me and we got her the care she needed. My mom was supposed to pass away. Baba minimized her suffering to that event that night.

****

Shree was going to a devotee's house in Sacramento and she invited me to come with her. A small group gathered. They wanted Baba to come so He did.

Baba began to show signs of chocking and I could see His throat swelling. I could also see the pain on His face. I couldn't watch. I started crying.

Baba produced a Lakshmi murti from His mouth.

After the murti came I asked Baba, "Why? Why do you have to do this? This pain and suffering...what's the need for this?"

He looked at me with so much love and compassion in His eyes. "This is what they want."

He's going through all that pain to satisfy a single desire that is in another soul. Who does that? She takes on the sicknesses of others. She has taken on my family problems. I have seen it over and over again. If two people have a problem in their family or otherwise, you will see that problem play out with Shree and another person. It is a lesson for the devotees.

Once I said to Baba, "You do some things just for fun. Just for fun."

"There is not a thing that I do just for fun," He said. "Everything is with a purpose and reason."

DONALD OLDS

As Sathya Sai Baba was dying Shree was lying in her bed. We had heard that morning from our Sai sources that Baba was not doing well. As Shree lie there she was going in and out of different worlds. We knew that from the things she said. Some of the Gurumukhs who Shirdi Sai Baba chose through the mandir in South San Francisco were there. A few were saying the mantras Baba had given them, and others were saying the Tryambakam. It may have been six or seven of us present. Shree's consciousness would sort of come into the room where her body was lying and then she would go out again. Shree was experiencing the death of Sathya Sai Baba. She would say things like. "I have an IV in my arm. They are shocking me now. I am in pain." Then finally she said, "He's not going to make it."

Some time later Inder (Pandher) got on the internet and she said Sathya Sai Baba had died.

****

James (Jagindar Prashad) was a part of the Raksha Bhadan celebration. Some of us came early and performed the ceremony with Shree. There were maybe thirteen of us, male and female. She went into her bedroom; came back out and walked straight up to Shirdi's chair without saying a word to anyone. Shree took Baba's clothes off the chair He gives darshan from and she put them on. Afterwards Shree told someone to get Baba another chair, and to put that chair in the middle of the room. So it was Baba, now, who came over and sat in the chair and crossed His leg.

This was like a different Baba, and the room felt more ethereal. There was a different presence at the time. I felt like I was in a different place, a place like Vaikuntha.

Once He sat down He had us sit in a big circle around Him, and He began to speak. I don't speak Hindi so I didn't understand but James was on my right interpreting and Inder was on my left filling in.

Baba had all the ladies come up and do the raksha bhadan with the ladies making Baba their brother. He started talking about the gopis and how the gopis were the sadhus of the previous age, male and female because sex doesn't matter with Baba. He mostly talked to the guys. He said, "You're my gopis."

At this point James was in tears. What Baba said was so emotionally strong. He said to Him it does not matter if we are male or female; we have been both in the past. Then Baba invited the guys who wanted to be his brother to come up. One by one they went up and performed some ceremonial movements. He gave them a fifty dollar bill, or two of them. Baba materialized them.

I was the last one left. I hesitated because I didn't know what to do.

"Do you want Baba to be your brother?" Inder asked.

I did want it and I went up and I knelt in front of Him. Baba began to tease me.

"I don't have any more money," He said. "I don't have any money for you and I am not going to give you any money."

In my heart I thought, *No money, I just love you.* "Baba, I don't mind," I replied.

"Okay, go ahead," He said. "Continue."

I thought about all the sages who sat in front of Vishnu who didn't know what to do, and in doing the wrong thing came back as insects. I had no idea what to do with the sandalwood paste, kumkum, orange sindoor or any of the ceremonial stuff.

"Baba, am I doing this right?"

He looked at me. "No."

No insect for me, I thought. *I'm going to be bacteria.*

"Continue," He said.

I go to give Him fruit and I dropped it on Him! Suddenly I thought, *Bacteria is too high. I'm going to be a virus.*

"Do the aarti," Baba instructed.

I picked up the plate and did the aarti.

"Do it three times."

I did as I was told.

When I was done Baba put His hand on the puja plate that had the various powders, fruit and such, and all of a sudden a fifty-dollar bill was there.

He gave that fifty dollars to me.

****

One time I felt so graced to be at the mandir and to meet Shree. I asked what did I do to have this kind of grace.

"He really doesn't like answering questions about your past," Shree told me when I mentioned it.

It was a sandwich night, and the next thing I know I'm sitting next to Baba.

He looked at me and asked, "Do you have any questions?"

"What did I do in the past for me to be able to be with you now?"

My thinking was, I wanted to continue to do what I did that allowed such grace.

He looked at me and said, "You were the sweeper. You are in the book." He pointed to everyone. "All of you have been written about."

I went home and pulled out my Satcharita; the slim red copy. There were three paragraphs about the sweeper. My name was Bala.

INDERJIT PANDHER

Through the years Baba has mentioned His Vishwaroop. At Shirdi Sai Baba's birthday celebration in 2012 I was graced to see It.

Baba would talk about how He intended to show His Vishwaroop to certain devotees, and in my mind it has always been that I wanted to see it. So I was looking at Baba during the celebration and the thought of how I wanted to see His Vishwaroop floated through my mind. Moments later I forgot about it. People continued to receive Baba's darshan and He was with some other devotees when all of a sudden I saw It! Just like Krishna's with all the heads. His Vishwaroop was right behind Him and I saw the entire group. It was a quick glance...but I saw It.

****

We decided to chant the Hanuman Chalissa for twenty-four hours. I was there for all of the chanting but I went downstairs right before the aarti and I fell asleep. They called me so I could be there but by the time I returned upstairs it was over. I missed the aarti. I felt really bad because the main way to reap the benefits of the chanting...of the prayer is to do aarti. I felt very bad. I cried.

I took mom (Shree) to the doctor the next day and we stopped in the parking lot of a vegetarian restaurant because mom was hungry. I started talking to mom about what happened. I started crying because I still felt very bad. As I cried I looked down and then I looked to the side where Mom sat and all of a sudden her face was just huge. It was a huge form of Hanuman! His checks were red and His lips were swollen and red. Both were tomato red. Hanuman's chin protruded and so did His eyes as He looked at me. It was the full form of Hanuman. I cried as I enjoyed that darshan, and I touched His feet. He was there for a good amount of time. I thanked Him and I spoke to Him about my not being there for aarti. He continued to look at me and finally He put His hand up and gave me a blessing before He left. Mom fainted immediately after that. As usual, after Hanuman gave darshan, her face was badly bruised for several days.

HANUMAN

SUN PARK

I was introduced to Sathya Sai Baba during the last years of His physical presence in Puttaparthi; at a time when He had basically stopped giving personal interviews. I wasn't deeply involved with Him and I dared to tell Baba, "If you do not plan to give me a personal interview then don't trouble me by calling me to Puttaparthi." Truth is I had no desire to go, and through His Grace He didn't call me. I had immigration issues at the time and perhaps if I didn't I would have approached it differently. I also thought Sathya Sai was going to live to ninety-six... not lunar calendar years but by the Gregorian calendar, the western calendar, so when He dropped His body in 2011 I felt He tricked us. Oh my goodness! I was the one who had told God I wished I was born when Jesus walked the earth! Thank God Prema Sai is coming. I realized how much I needed this kind of physical connection.

Not long after that I was told about Shree in South San Francisco and how Shirdi Baba came there. I asked my boyfriend, Sean Dee, and Ganesh (Reynel Ruiz) to go with me the first time I went there. That night we felt as if ninety percent of the darshan was for me, and when I kneeled before Baba tears flowing from my eyes, Baba said, "You did not get to see me in the body in Puttaparthi , but you are getting to see me here."

After getting Swami's physical darshan in such a way He gave me step-by-step instructions of how to resolve my immigration issues.

****

In 2012 Sean and I were graced with Shree staying in our home for one week. After we picked her up from the LAX airport on June 30th, I had to work for four hours, and one of the things Sean and Shree did to occupy the time was walk and explore our neighborhood. On the way Sean picked a beautiful pink hibiscus and when they returned to the house he offered it to Baba, where we always make our offerings, in front of a huge photo of Sathya Sai Baba. Not long after that they picked me up from work. When we entered my house I noticed the beautiful flower.

"Wait a minute. Is that vibhuti on Baba's picture?" Shree asked as I gazed at the hibiscus.

Sean and I looked at Shirdi Sai Baba's photograph and there was a chunk of vibhuti on His mouth. And the vibhuti was still coming. My mouth dropped open because four nights before I had dreamed of Baba. He was very huge in the South San Francisco mandir and He was manifesting kum kum from His mouth. The kumkum turned to a rose and He threw that rose onto my lap. When I saw the vibhuti on Baba's mouth I knew it was related to my recent dream.

And then Shree said, "That is my favorite picture."

Of all the photos that we have of Baba the vibhuti was coming on Shree's favorite Shirdi Sai Baba photo. He wanted us to be clear it was Shirdi Sai's energy.

The maya is strong when it comes to Shree and Baba. Before Shree stayed with us that week Baba tested us about six months before. I was not a gurumukh at the time and we literally arrived to pick her up on January 5, 2012, when she was in the LA area and she did not end up coming with us. Sean had called me and said, "Your love, Shree...Baba has come." When I looked at my phone I realized she had attempted to call me several times as well, reaching out to us at a time when she was in distress. So I prepared the house with a runner made from a sari I received from Sathya Sai Baba, and I decorated the mandir with flowers and made other preparations...but she didn't come that time and Sean and I were okay with that. Because we were sincerely okay, we knew we had passed the test. Baba always tests you.

So this time, when Shree came, I did not make the same level of preparations. I decorated the mandir with flowers but that was it because Shree begged us to take her away from all that. She said one of the reasons she loved us was because we treated her like a regular human being. Sean really wanted to honor that and he kept saying to me, "No bhajans. No mention of Shirdi or anything like that." When I placed flowers in my mandir that day I was kind of thinking I was accepting Shree...not Baba. Because Shree was pleading with us, "Come and get me. I love you guys because you treat me like a regular human being."

So we assured her we would do regular fun things. There was a full moon that night and we went to a ceremony where we howled and just had fun with some other people. But somehow, the second day, out-of-the-blue things changed.

"Shree, I hate to say this but...there is one person who would just lo-ove to see you," Sean told her.

This was so strange. Usually it would be me that would have said something like that, but Sean said it, and I thought, 'Okay, Baba. You have made this so smooth. You have said, 'Sean, you say this'.

Shree said, "Ohhh, Ganesh. Ganesh is no problem."

So we called Ganesh several times and left a message. He replied with a message, "No, no. I can't come. I just can't travel with you."

Sean responded with a voicemail, "There is such a big surprise for you."

While Sean was leaving the voicemail, he saw Ganesh was calling him. Ganesh told him he had placed a flower on Baba's photo in the Malibu Temple, his phone started ringing and immediately the flower starting dancing. The picture and the flower started dancing! Ganesh said he thought, 'I must call him back. I must call him! This is something related to Baba.'

"We have a big surprise for you," Sean said when they spoke. "So whenever you can Sunday or Monday, whatever...come."

"Okay, "Ganesh said, "Tuesday evening is good."

We decided to have some food.

"Bring some Indian spice pickles," I said, because Shree wanted them. Ganesh is a wonderful cook. He said he would definitely come because Baba was telling him to, and that he would bring a couple of dishes.

We have held bhajans at our place many times, and so we rehearsed with Shree what would happen when Ganesh came, choosing a place where she would hide. When Ganesh came, he brought this beautiful silver tray with great things to eat, and we convinced him to sit on the floor with his eyes closed, and we began to sing, Jagadambe. Shree went and stood in front of him at that time and began to pour vibhuti on Ganesh's head.

"Open your eyes, Ganesh," we said.

His mouth dropped open when he saw Shree, and because of the bhajan Baba started to come. We were at a total lost as to what to do.

Quickly we said, "Aarti! Aarti!" ... or else! We tried to stop Baba from coming. We weren't prepared. No robe. No hookah. Nothing. Shree had warned us it could be dangerous. This was Shirdi Baba. Not Sathya. He could be furious.

Shree Sai Baba said to Ganesh, "You said you were not coming to San Francisco, but this time San Francisco came to you."

Ganesh never told Shree he was not going back to South San Francisco.

This whole thing opened Ganesh's eyes.

"Are you still not coming?" Shree asked.

"I am coming," Ganesh replied.

****

The day after we surprised Ganesh by Shree's presence at our house, with some pleading from Ganesh; he said he would cook for her and we promised no bhajans ; Shree agreed to go to Ganesh's for dinner. Before we left I plucked a beautiful yellow hibiscus and placed it on the silver tray Ganesh had given us. Shree watched all of this. Sean drove and Shree sat in the passenger seat. I sat behind her.

The energy was joyous because we were remarking about how happy Ganesh was going to be, and all of a sudden, in the middle of the conversation, Baba comes. He turned toward me. "Why fear when I am here?"

And bam...I'm smelling vibhuti! 'What just happened?' I thought. The voice that said 'Why fear when I am here?" was Baba's voice! Shree's voice is quite different.

I turned all this over in my mind. *Baba said these words to me and now I am smelling vibhuti! I never knew I had fear inside of me...maybe deep inside of me. I began to repeat. Om Sai Ram. Om Sai Ram.*

"Guys, I'm sorry," I said to Sean and Shree, who came back right after Baba's words, "I think I'm going to have to turn on the light inside of this car."

"Okay," they said.

As Sean continued to drive I turned on the light. I looked down at the flower, and on the tray that I was holding there was a chunk of vibhuti.

"Guys! Vibhuti!" Then I said to Shree, "Baba popped out of you. I'm so sorry."

"What did He say," she asked because Shree does not know what Baba says or does.

"Why fear when I am here. And until now, I never knew that I had fear really deep down inside of me. Any anxiety...any worry. I never knew fear related to that." I meant I knew it but those things were not on the surface of my life."

After the vibhuti came I said, " I want to keep this flower."

"Don't be greedy," Sean replied. "This one may be meant for Ganesh's new Shirdi Sai Baba murti."

You see, Ganesh's new statue had not been given abhishekam yet.

"When you plucked the flower," Sean said, "didn't you have the intention of giving it to Ganesh?"

"Yes," I replied, "that's true but Swami gave it to me."

This kind of exchange went on back and forth between us.

We arrived at Ganesh's, Shree got out of the car and said, "Sweetie, don't worry. I know how much you love Baba. Forget about this conversation and simply enjoy this moment. This is for you. When it comes to Baba I am like you. Holding on to Baba. Baba is mine."

With so much love being expressed by Shree about Baba my heart opened. I heard what I wanted to hear and my heart knew...now I can give it to Ganesh. So I poured the vibhuti that manifested on the hibiscus on Ganesh's Shirdi Sai Baba murti. I performed abhishekam. It was all very beautiful.

Ganesh really wanted us to do a few bhajans in his mandir. We did...and Baba came. I couldn't help but remember how Shree had warned it could be dangerous if Baba comes and you are not prepared. She even told us of particular incidents when Baba came and was furious. So here Sean, Ganesh and I sat, and Baba had come.

We knelt down in front of Him.

"Do not tell my daughter," He said. "She will be very upset. I will make it easy for you after I leave. But I had to come. I had to come and bless you. All of your desires will be fulfilled."

Ganesh had some items with which we dressed Baba. One thing I was very aware of was how shaky Sean was. He's a big man, but I have never seen him so nervous. Immediately after we dressed Baba Sean began to apologize.

"Baba, we are so sorry. So sorry. We didn't mean to call you. We don't have your hookah .... We didn't prepare well."

But Baba put us at ease. "I had to come to bless you."

At our house after we sang Jagadambe Baba was there perhaps seventy-five percent. This time He was fully there. Shree was in a complete trance.

"I want jao," He said.

Jao, I thought. *What the heck is jao?*

Thank God Sean knew, and we gave Baba water. So much happened. It was an amazing experience.

After we returned to our house Shree asked, "Why does my body feel like this? Why does it feel so heavy? I know this feeling."

"Baba did not come," I replied.

It was very difficult for me to lie, but what I hold on to is Baba's words. He told me to say it. Whoever says whatever I am not going to listen to. He told me to lie to her...I lied.

But Sean, he couldn't help it.

"Sister," he said, "Baba came." And I pinched him.

"What?" Shree said. "What happened?"

"No, no, no," I told her, "Baba did not come."

Shree excused herself and went to the bathroom and Sean and I had some words about it. Ultimately I told him we are obeying Baba. When Shree joined us, once more she asked if Baba came, and Sean and I reminded her of how we had hiked a few days before. We said what she was feeling was a result of the hiking.

"So why don't you shower and relax," I suggested.

"No," Shree replied. "I know this feeling and I do not want to wash off this energy. I am going to just rest as it is."

****

The last day Shree spent in my home Shree and I relaxed on the bed. I thought about the darshans Baba had given to me, Sean and Ganesh. I thought, *Baba you partially came in my home when we sang Jagadambe, and you fully came in Ganesh's mandir when we sang bhajans. I know you partially came in my home because we didn't want Shree to go through it. But now Swami...if it is okay with you...I would like for you to fully come in my home before she leaves. It hurts me to even think like this for Shree's sake, and I am torn, but I do want you to come.*

I meditated on Baba in this way as Shree was lying on the bed and my boyfriend, Sean, was showering.

"Oh Baba this is the last morning before we leave. Om Sai

Ram. Om Sai Ram," I said it within me with all my heart.

All of a sudden Shree got up and sat on the side of the bed. I watched as she positioned herself in what I call the "phone call Baba" pose. He had His face resting on His hand with His knee raised. It is how He appears in Shree's favorite photo of Baba.

There Baba sat, and I had no doubt He had come because I longed for it. When I looked at Shree's face...it was completely Baba.

When Baba spoke He said, "This is the last day of Me staying here with you. Some people take Me as a joke. Only for those who know who truly I Am can have this kind of relationship. But this is who I Am. I Am no joke."

Those words tattooed on my mind...on my heart.

Directly after He spoke Baba began to motion His hand like Sathya Sai Baba. Very fast. Round and round, and a chunk of vibhuti came right away.

I was in total awe! I was trying to think of what to do. I thought should I give Him a scarf...turban...I mean....

By then Sean came out of the shower and positioned himself for meditation, because that's what we do in the morning.

Baba motioned to him.

Quickly I went over to Sean," Come, come, come."

Sean got up and received Baba's darshan and a little of the vibhuti.

"This is my last day, but I am always with you. And now I am going to rest a little bit," Baba said before He left.

After that Shree slept for about twenty minutes.

"Baba came," I said when she woke up.

"Oh really?"

"Yes! Look at your palm."

There was evidence of the vibhuti that had been there. But speaking honestly, I had removed as much vibhuti as was humanly possible and secured it away. This was such a special darshan for me.

We celebrated Gurupurnima the next day in the South San Francisco mandir, and when Baba came He called me to Him right away.

"It was never Shree," He said. " It was never my daughter. It was me all along. I lived with you. I slept with you. I am always with you. I love you very much."

And then Swami made the face that I make when I am indicating to people that Baba has come on Shree. When He comes for the darshans in the mandir her mouth turns downward and Baba's face appears longer with this very downward turned mouth, and I motion downward with my hands and turn my mouth down to tell others that Baba has come.

Baba made that face and said, "No, no, no. It was Me all along. Never my daughter."

So the Maya came here and there while Shree visited us, and the truth is Baba came to us in the form of Shree playing the Maya.

****

We were preparing for the ride to San Francisco and we rented a car. We went to the rental company and Baba gave us this beautiful car for an amazing price.

Just for fun I said, "Let me google and find out the kind of car Sathya Sai rides in." I knew He had many kinds of cars, and during Shirdi Baba's time people were not driving.

So I typed Sathya Sai Baba cars into Google and a photograph of Baba standing by a car that was the same color and shape as the car we had rented popped up. Of all the cars that Swami has ridden in. Swami kept indicating the one you are next to is not Shree. It is Me.

As soon as we began to drive to South San Francisco fireworks began!

At one point Shree said, "Look at that! Look at that," although her basic demeanor throughout the ride was calm and serene.

When she said that I replied, "They know who's riding. Swami is doing this."

Although I said that, the conscious part of me kept thinking *this is Shree riding with us.* The fireworks continued to go off as we drove on Hwy 101.

Still, Sean, Ganesh and I had already determined if Baba should come while we drove to South San San Francisco, this time we would be prepared. So we had a robe, His hookah, paan, but amazing Baba…. This time Shree spent the majority of the trip on the telephone with her family addressing personal matters.

****

Directly after we arrived at Ganesh's place in North Hollywood, Shree looked around and said, "What about a new chair for Baba? Can we get a chair like that for Baba?"

The chair Ganesh has for Baba is similar to the one Sathya Sai sat on in India. And, most of Sai centers have it.

Before I could speak Ganesh volunteered right away.

"Bring it as soon as possible for Baba," Shree said.

Ganesh knew where he could get the chair Shree Sai Baba wanted. It was made by the same person who made Sathya Sai's chair in India.

Within three weeks we were ready to take Baba's new chair to South San Francisco. Right before our delivery date Sean invited Dick Selby, and he volunteered to use his van for the mission.

Dick was uncertain if Baba would like it. "If not, we will just bring it back."

But, I Knew it was Baba's WILL to have a new throne exactly looking like Sathya Sai's in India.

Along with this beautiful leela of His, there was a tremendous blessing for all of us. Ganesh and I had Birthdays just one week apart, and we both secretly wanted to celebrate our birthdays with Baba's presence. We took the chair on July 26th. My birthday is July 22nd. Ganesh's birthday is July 29th. Amazing Baba.

When we arrived at Shree's house, for the first time in her life, she sat down on Baba's chair as Shree. She said she had never done it before and never would. But we all wanted to make sure Baba would be comfortable with this new chair, so we asked her to sit down. And then...right away Baba started coming into her. She tried to fight it by getting up but couldn't. The lower half of her body would not move. We all rushed to help her get up her from the chair.

"Baba is coming," Parvati Ma said. "He likes that new chair."

Finally Baba came during bhajans that evening. He called me right away.

"Do you like it?" He asked.

"It? What is it, Baba?"

"This chair."

"Oh yes Baba. Ganesh brought it for you with his love and devotion to you. We all just came along with Your grace."

"No, it is Me who brought it here...for you. You have never seen me in Puttaparthi. So I have brought it here for you to see me on this chair."

My jaw just dropped and I started to cry.

That night after darshan, many people talked and said, 'Tonight He was Sathya Sai.'

In the middle of the public darshan Baba told Bakul Patel and Ashu (Asish Chandra) to make sure He had His handkerchief on the arms of His chair, and He motioned like Sathya Sai, circling His hand for protection.

Alas He fulfilled my desire to see Him as Sathya Sai in Puttaparthi.

BAKUL PATEL

I started coming to the mandir in South San Francisco in 2003. I didn't want to come because it was on a Thursday and I wanted to stay home, but thankful to my dad he kept pushing me and pushing me.

Back then it wasn't like it is today...how Baba comes every week. Baba came, perhaps, once a month at the time, and there were perhaps less than twenty people attending. The first time I saw Baba "come" I was sitting in the back, and I didn't really believe it. I watched him take out pendants. I watched him take out vibhuti and I thought...*This is probably fake.* I didn't believe it one bit.

After three or four months it was Baba's birthday, and because someone in the Lal family had passed away they couldn't hold the large celebration in the mandir, so it was held in Hayward, California at the home of one of Shree's cousins. I wasn't as close to Baba as I am now. I sat down far in the back, and I saw Him take out pendants and this and that, and I said to myself... in my head, *If you really are who you say you are... The Almighty, I want you to call me up and give me a pendant out of a flower.* The moment I said it...the moment the thought ran through my mind, Baba turned, looked at me, and pointed at me.

"You. Come up."

Rather shocked I got up and went to Him.

Without a single word He took a flower and manifested a Shiva pendant for me. I was instantly scared. I had goosebumps all over me, and after that day...after that experience, I knew there was something in South San Francisco. Something bigger than what I could see. That drove me to come every Thursday, and that is how my bond became stronger with Baba, Shree and the family. That experience made me excited to come to the mandir although I still sat in the back. I enjoyed the energetics of the bhajans and Baba's darshan. He began to play games with me and I would pray to Him all the time. I would say "Baba keep me close to you. Keep me close. If I am fortunate enough, keep me close." Eventually He told me to always be the one to light His 'chillum'.

****

Being physically close to Baba when He "comes" I am so grateful to be close to God. From flowers I have seen Him pull out pendants, rudraksh, bracelets and necklaces. I have also seen Him manifest four or five Shivalingams from His mouth.

Once, while we were relaxing in the house downstairs, Shree said she felt like she was going to throw up; out of her mouth came this small Lakshmi murti. People don't believe it when you tell them. You have to see it to believe it. That is my motto.

****

When Baba gives darshan He tells me lots of things, sometimes

about people's physical conditions and even foretelling death...
and it happens. That's how I know whatever He says comes
true.

DAHYABHAI D. PATEL

On the third day of my first visit to Puttaparthi in 2003, I sat in Kulwant Hall as everyone prepared for Baba's appearance. There was an empty cushion beside me, and I wondered who placed it there. Soon a very interesting man sat down. He held my hand and told me all about myself. One of the last things he said was, "Forget about India. Go to the United States. You can worship Baba there." After a few minutes the cushion was empty.

During one of my return trips to India Baba sent me on a hunt for a particular place, and because I didn't know where to go, after some advise, I hired a driver to go into this particular jungle where this church was located. "Baba is there," I was told.

I noticed the hall was very small and I asked who came there. I was told a lot of people come because of Baba's miracles that occur. They also told me they wanted to sell the house next door so they could build a bigger hall for prayer. On the spot I committed to send the money that was needed to build that hall. There was a time when Baba told us to volunteer and help when we could. I made a commitment to myself to do that.

We were in the States with a group of people, years later, and they began to talk about South San Francisco. I asked my friend, Mayuri Dalal, about the mandir. She knew about it and offered to take us there. It was Shivaratri 2007.

My wife and I went up to Baba and He created this beautiful gold bracelet for my wife that had Hanuman, Shiva and Ganesh on it.

I started attending that mandir and one day I said, "Swami, why don't you come to my place?"

"If you come every week, I will come," He said.

From that time on I have attended every week, and I volunteer to help the Lal family in every way that I can. We were given a murti of Baba from the mandir after Baba advised Shree to do so. Baba's miracles occur on that murti.

In 2010 Shree shared with me that they wanted to do some remodeling inside the mandir. As part of their plans an announcement was made after bhajans that Thursday. Part of the remodeling plans included creating a new silver chair for Shirdi Sai Baba's murti, which is the focus of the mandir.

I don't know what happened but before I knew it my hand was in the air. "I will take care of it," I volunteered. "Whatever the costs. Whatever the problem. I will take care of it."

But soon it was made clear that other devotees wanted to donate toward the chair as well, and it became a collaborative effort.

Several times I went and measured to make sure we had the right dimensions.

I contacted a friend in India. I told him about the project and how we wanted a manufacturer that we could trust with such a precious undertaking. I gave my friend a list of the items that would be needed to make the chair. I told him to present the list to the man who I formed a relationship with when I bought the land for the prayer hall years before. My friend did as I asked, and to my surprise that man was an engineer. Not only was he an engineer, but he said he was always called to do things for Baba in Puttaparthi, including making furniture. That man is the one who made the silver chair for Baba's murti in South San Francisco. Baba laid the foundation for the South San Francisco connection many years before it happened.

****

I was at the Lal's house doing some repairs when I took time out to sit and talk with Shree. We were alone.

"What are you doing, Shree?" I asked

"Dad, I am studying," she replied. "I have to pass the test."

Suddenly Shree's face was gone and in its place was Shirdi Sai Baba's face! Totally.

"What is going on, Shree?!"

"No-no-no," she said and the moment was gone.

SHUMADIBEN PATEL

During my first darshan of Baba in South San Francisco He gave me a beautiful gold bracelet with three lockets on it. Hanuman, Shiva and Ganesh were the Gods on the lockets. I was crying so much when I went before Him. My heart was full and I was thinking about Shiva. Shiva's image was on the center locket of the bracelet. Baba took a carnation and rubbed it rapidly between His fingers. He kept rubbing and rubbing and rubbing and then the bracelet started coming out. It kept coming and coming and coming. I don't remember feeling anything accept for the feeling that I was with Baba.

****

We joined the Lal family when they celebrated Diwali in 2007. When we went up to the house there were no lights and for a moment my husband, Dahayabhai D. Patel, and I thought we had the wrong date. Then Amma (Parvati Lal) opened the door.

"Come in. Come in," she invited us. "There are no lights."

After we were inside Baba came. He instructed us, "Light candles. This is like Shirdi now."

Mind you, there were no lights. No music. Nothing.

Baba talked about so many things and I actually felt as if I was in Shirdi. It felt different there that day.

Sunil Patel, an engineer, tried to figure out what was wrong with the electricity but he found nothing. It was so strange, because all the other houses on the street had electricity but the Lal house did not. After we sang a few bhajans and came downstairs from the mandir the electricity came on.

****

In 2011 I attended bhajans at the mandir and I sat in one of the chairs in the back. I heard a sound like footsteps. I looked at the window that was not far away and I saw the original Shirdi Sai Baba dressed in His white clothing. He was using the slates of the window blinds for steps. It looked as if He was coming into the mandir.

****

Around 2010 Justin Lal bought a dog and they named him Oreo. Baba told Justin to buy that dog. Baba said when He was in Shirdi He had a dog named Hira, and that Oreo was Hira.

Some time later I came down with a cold and I decided not to go to bhajans one Thursday. I didn't want anyone else to become sick.

I prayed to Baba as I lie in my bed, when all of a sudden it looked as if the night-time had turned to daylight. I decided to go into my garden to see. I got up and I had to go through my garage. In my garage there was an empty box by the door, but when I looked in it I saw Oreo! He was going round and round.

Surprised I said, "Oreo? How are you?"

"Fine." I heard Oreo reply.

Can you imagine my surprise? "Oreo! How are you?"

"Fine. Fine." He replied. "Good luck," he said before he disappeared.

Shree has said that Baba will come through animals if He wills it.

SNEHA PATEL

During the early times of my joining the temple, seva to the homeless, "sandwich night", occurred two Fridays a month, and major functions (Maha Shivaratri, Shirdi Baba's Birthday and Sathya Baba's Birthday) were celebrated on Saturdays. It was during one of these celebrations that I experienced certain miracles that were personal to me and my family.

As usual, Thursday we had regular bhajans and as is usual during major functions, many of Shree's extended family flew in a couple of days early from various locations to squeeze in a Thursday bhajan before the main celebration on Saturday. My family was no exception. I had six members of my extended family who came. Baba gave each and every one a darshan and spent a little extra time with the ones visiting from out of town.

The next day was Friday and happened to be sandwich night. This particular Friday we decided to give care packages along with the sandwiches to the homeless. There were a lot of people there to help since Shree's family from out of town were staying with her, and I brought my family plus my extended family from out of town. Others dropped in just to be included in seva or show their support. We set up the sandwich assembly line in the usual spot at the kitchen counter, and we sectioned off a different area of the house to create an assembly line for the care packages. We put toiletry items like a toothbrush, toothpaste, soap, socks, etc. into big ziploc bags. It was very busy and festive.

Everyone was in good spirits doing what they could to help and do service.

Shree sat on a sofa overseeing everything and joking around with everyone. I was aware of when she got up and went into the bathroom. When the bathroom door opened, we noticed it was not Shree who came out. It was Sathya Baba! For a few moments He looked around in approval of all the seva that was being done. He motioned for everyone to continue doing their work even though our natural response was to stop and prostrate at His feet.

As I continued to watch Him, He looked as if He was choking. At that time Baba was manifesting murtis through the mouth, but when this took place we really didn't know what was happening. He looked as if He was really struggling.

I thought, *Oh My Gosh! Baba is struggling so much! Why does He have to do this for us?!* It is not easy to watch someone struggling in this manner and not be able to help. Your heart goes out. If you have seen Sathya Sai Baba go through this process in Puttaparthi, then you know exactly what I mean.

After much angst, a lingam came out of His mouth. Shree's husband, Dhiren, was there to receive the lingam in his hands. Dhiren was instructed to walk around with the lingam so that everyone could see it, and have darshan of it. If I recall correctly it was brownish, tan in color, and longer than the others Baba had manifested. It reminded me of an elongated thumb.

Each lingam was very different, special and unique. Maybe

one had an outline of Baba's face or what looked like a third eye. I have personally seen several of the twelve or so lingams produced. It was very powerful.

After the lingam incident, Dhiren was instructed to have five people go up into the temple to find a flask containing amrit. The five people went up and noticed a flask that previously held manifested wine had not only changed to amrit…it was overflowing with amrit!

Baba directed Dhiren to give everyone present a taste of it, and also to give a small sample to each family to take home to share with their family. Following Baba's direction, Dhiren prepared some containers with the amrit and each family received one container. Although my niece's family was not in the U.S. at the time, she got one too. This was her first time at the temple and she was very excited about what she had seen and experienced. She told me she was going to share the amrit with her friends.

The vibrations were very high from the seva and what had taken place with the lingam and amrit. In the middle of the excitement my niece lost her container. We looked around and found one and we gave it to her. By the time it was time to leave my niece had lost her amrit again! That's when we informed her of the importance of Baba's words. Baba had said to share it with your family and she had intended to share it with her friends.

****

I went to India in 2007. We traveled to Shirdi and a couple of other temples. It was four of us, Shree, her mom's sister, Asha Auntie, Dhiren and me. During one of the car rides Shree wore a nice, silver ring she had purchased. It was a Baba ring. Asha

Auntie admired Shree's ring. She was not so happy with a ring of Baba that she had purchased. She tried Shree's ring on and after a few minutes Shree wanted her ring back. Asha Auntie didn't want to give it back and said so. While they were arguing about the ring we stopped at an ice cream shop. As we sat outside Shree began to look over here and over there. She could see Baba. He was playing hide and seek with her as she leaned this way and that. According to Shree they had this conversation:

"Do you like that ring?" Baba asked.
"Yes I like that ring."
"Do you want that ring?"
"Yes, I want that ring!"
"Are you sure you want that ring?" Baba teased.

All of a sudden "poof" one manifested in Shree's hand. It was the exact same ring that her aunt had on. Now they both had the same ring. Shree had one that was manifested by Baba.

By that time I had seen some miracles happen and I started laughing because it was so cool. Playing like He usually plays. He is very playful with Shree and all of a sudden there it was.

****

It was a Thursday, bhajan day. We went to the mandir and Shree was wearing a neck brace. She could hardly move and was in much pain. Come to find out she had fallen down from the top of the stairs and thrown out her neck and back. Shree's room was upstairs, but ever since the accident she had been staying downstairs because it was too painful to climb up and down the stairs. She needed help getting up, getting dressed, getting around, going to the bathroom, etc. The fall happened on a Monday so she had suffered like this for four days.

When it was time for bhajans, two of the brothers carried

Shree upstairs and, of course, Baba didn't come because she was in too much pain. Afterwards a couple of the brothers carried her back downstairs.

Later on we discussed what was going on and Shree told us Baba had taken another devotee's pain. She was suffering through this pain from someone else's karma. Baba was protecting another one of His devotees.

We all offered to take a little bit of the pain amongst other suggestions to help her. In the course of that discussion Baba came.

One very persuasive brother asked Baba to please take away Shree's pain. He said she was such a good person and didn't deserve to go through all this pain. While this brother pleaded with Him it was obvious Baba had no issues from the injuries. He was not in pain at all.

Baba listened carefully before He said, "That is what she is meant to do."

But the brother continued to ask Baba to remove Shree's pain. It went back and forth, back and forth for some time.

Finally, Baba said, "I will do it on one condition. Do you all agree?"

Everyone agreed. Mind you, none of us knew what we were agreeing to.

Baba repeated, "Everyone has to agree to the one condition. Do you all agree?"

Excitedly we all agreed again. We had persuaded Baba! But what did we agree to?

After a long pause, Baba said, "Exercise. Everyone has to exercise."

We all followed Baba upstairs into the temple area to exercise. Although Baba was in no pain He still had a few of the brothers carefully carry Him up the stairs. Baba is very heavy when He comes. When Baba arrived upstairs He took off the neck brace and was supple and full of energy.

"Who is going to lead?" He asked.

Someone suggested stretches and bends and other things.

Baba said, "This is how it was in Shirdi when all the devotees gathered together. It was a happy time. You were all there in Shirdi. We should have a sleep over one day just like in Shirdi's time."

Baba made jokes too. "What do you get when you add an 'ah' to your ghor (leg)? It becomes ghora (horse)."

We had lots of fun and enjoyed the time we got to spend with Baba.

"Don't worry, I'm going to take the pain away before I leave," He promised. "Don't worry, she'll be fine."

When our exercise time with Baba came to an end Baba asked if anyone had any questions. He answered a few questions before He asked if He could leave. We all agreed that we had kept Baba long enough and allowed Him to do so.

After Baba left Shree was perfectly fine. She had no more pain and was very happy to be back to normal.

****

The pain woke me up Thursday morning, April 30, 2009 around 1:30 A.M. It radiated back towards my shoulder blades. I thought it was heartburn. By the time my husband, Sunil, woke up, around 5:30 a.m., he found me sitting in the family room, in pain. Sunil suggested that I go to the emergency room, but I sent him to the pharmacy for heartburn medicine. Around twelve hours later I couldn't take the pain anymore and we went to the ER.

If you have ever been to an ER room you know there is always a wait, but not this time. There was no one there! The triage nurse and the admissions nurse, in sequence, asked all sorts of questions before another nurse came. I was registered and in a room within about ten minutes.

They gave me morphine for the pain; conducted a battery of tests and finally did an ultrasound. The ultrasound revealed I had gallstones! The doctor who attended me recommended I stay overnight and told me a surgeon would come and visit me in the morning. Although I was totally against having surgery, I wanted to try some alternative methods first; the doctor assured me it wouldn't hurt to just listen to what the surgeon had to say. In the end, it would be my decision.

When the surgeon talked to me the next day he assured me it would be a simple laparoscopic procedure. Three holes would be made and then he would just vacuum...suck out the gallbladder and that would take care of it. I would be released within a day or two. He felt if I didn't have it then I might have to have an emergency operation later. It would be better to do it on our terms.

Even though I was against the surgery, for my family the timing was perfect. Our insurance was scheduled to expire at the end of May, and my sister-in-law, who was visiting from India, was available and graciously volunteered to move in and take care of the kids. My husband was between contracts so he would not have to take off from work, and it seemed like it would just be the most convenient time to have the surgery. There was absolutely nothing preventing me from doing it! Darn it! So I reluctantly agreed to the laparoscopic procedure....

During my first conversation with the doctor after the surgery he said, "You are a very special lady!"

I smiled inside because I knew that the whole ordeal, as much as I hated it, was divinely orchestrated! It turned out that he was unable to sufficiently get all of the gallbladder out laparoscopically because there was too much scarring. He had to perform surgery the old fashion way to remove it. The doctor was amazed that I had not noticed or complained earlier about my gallbladder. He explained to me that our organs inside are very soft and silky. While he was moving everything aside to get to the gallbladder area he felt something hard. He investigated and found part of my intestine was black and hard. He ended up cutting out a foot of my intestine along with removing my gallbladder. If my intestine issue would have gone undetected; it would have caused much bigger problems down the road. It was truly a blessing in disguise. By the time any symptoms would have surfaced, my body might have had too many toxins in it. The one to two day hospital stay turned into a ten day stay. I went from taking care of everyone in my family to completely surrendering and allowing people to take care of me.

The day before Mother's Day, 2009 I was released from the hospital. Throughout this ordeal I never doubted Baba was watching over me and orchestrated the whole thing. While I was in the hospital Shree visited me, and it was nice to have her come. Eventually during a conversation after I was released she told me that one of my nurses was Baba himself!

SUNIL PATEL

In June 2006 I dropped by Shree's house. There was work being done on the windows upstairs in the mandir and I wanted to help. Later I came downstairs and Shree was just sitting there. Her mom (Parvati Lal) was there as well.

"Look who's here," her mom said.

I looked… and it was Hanuman.

This was the first time I had ever seen Hanuman besides looking at pictures or statues! Her face had definitely changed. *Wow*, I thought. *This is amazing.*

We know about Hanuman but there He was sitting in real form. At first He was very quiet. There were no words exchanged. Suddenly He said. "Do you want to see what's in my chest?"

"No," I quickly said. "That's okay." I knew how Rama and Sita were in Hanuman's chest, but I just didn't want Him to open up His heart. It was very profound. You hear about these "legends" but it is really something to see One. It gives you confidence in the divine aspect.

****

It was Thursday bhajans, January, 2013. I was doing my usual meditation, as I sat in the back of the bhajan hall on a chair. A Baba devotee, who once lived in Puttaparthi and who sings from the heart, began to sing. I felt the vibration in the room get higher as I followed the bhajan and an incredible vein of energy went through me. Suddenly, I smelled jasmine flowers, which normally accompany Baba. This blessing energy coursed through me for the longest time. I felt a live current of electrifying energy in the right side of my body. Space expanded, and I felt a presence in front of me. There was this wonderful flow from that presence toward me. Baba gave darshan, through Shree, shortly after.

Some time after that experience I realized earlier that day I asked for a definitive experience. I said, "Show me your presence and your love. Show me your divine connection…the Divine connection."

****

During a bhajan in March 2013, Baba came and gave darshan. I was once again engaged in my usual meditation. At some point I noticed he created a rudraksh from a flower for someone. I thought of the power of intention. How clear your intention must be to manifest something instantly. A few minutes later Baba pointed toward me as He was blessing another devotee. He directed a flower toward me and as He threw it I saw a rudraksh drop out of that flower. The flower did not reach me and the rudraksh landed in another devotee's space. Immediately I told the devotee the rudraksh was for me. He gave it up somewhat reluctantly. Usually I would not have bothered. But because twice Baba pointed at me I knew the rudraksh had to come to me. I held it and felt the expansion and vibration.

The following Sunday, March 10th, a Shivaratri celebration was scheduled, but it was canceled because of a death in Shree's family. I had scheduled a massage with a friend who does massages that day. This friend has the ability to see beyond the veil of the physical plane.

As he worked on me he said someone was standing in the room.

"The person is small in height. He has Afro hair. He is smiling."

My friend said the man gestured...indicated that there was a stone that should be put in the hand and near the altar.

I told my friend to ask Him what does he want?

He expressed I had made a shift, and He was happy with the progress I was making. He then went to my altar and my friend said the entire altar lit up with a brilliant white light.

I knew Baba was referring to the rudraksh. My friend knew nothing about the rudraksh I had received that previous Thursday.

LYNN PENTZ

Some say, no one hears about…much less visits…the mandir of Shirdi Sai Baba of South San Francisco unless Baba personally invites you. Well, I'd certainly say that is true in my case.

In the summer of 2011, in downtown South San Francisco, I stood in a line that wrapped around the corner, waiting to pick up my renewed passport. Given I was contemplating a spiritual journey to India that I really couldn't afford, I thought it was a lovely coincidence – and maybe even a 'sign' that I stood next to a woman and her daughter dressed in Indian attire. We struck up a conversation that would change my life.

At one point the mother confidently confided, "You don't need to go all the way to Shirdi to see Sai Baba, Lynn. Sai Baba has come to you. Just like in Shirdi, he resides in South San Francisco".

Intrigued and delighted, I celebrated their whisperings about the same miracles, manifestations and spiritual energy that I knew occurred at Baba's Samadhi in Shirdi, and in southern India. They said the very same and more happened upstairs at a home temple in South San Francisco. It happened through and around an amazing woman named Shree, who Baba literally embodied while he gave darshan (blessings). The little girl in line then opened her wallet and gave me a blessed flower her grandfather gave her, and a packet of vibhuti that they explained regularly materialized from the feet of the life-size murti of Shirdi Sai Baba that resided in the front of the temple. As if filled with Baba's love overflowing, I received their blessings and the phone number of the grandfather who told me more and gave me the address.

Thursday, guru day in India, came. I heard the joyful bhajans as I approached the two-story residence and placed my shoes in a sacred trust amidst at least 100 others in front of the door. My mind dissolved as I walked up the stairs in eager anticipation of meeting the incomparable Shree while trying to grapple with the possibility that I might also, somehow, actually get to speak with the great immortal saint I had loved from afar, this lifetime, since 1973.

Every cell in my body pranamed (bowed) and jumped for joy as I turned the corner and was welcomed into a little piece of heaven straight out of India with magnificent life-size murtis of Durga and Shiva on each side of the smiling Baba statue I'd been told about.

I was kind of glad Baba didn't actually 'come through' Shree that first night as there was so much to take in. Being in the temple was miracle enough, and I met Shree and the family who I have come to adore.

I was awe struck not only by the refined, intense spiritual energy and the loveliness of the people, but, in particular, by the quality of reverence and exquisite care I witnessed Baba's assistant, Ashu, (Asish Chandra) demonstrate as he unfolded Baba's white attire and gently placed it on the large chair where

Shree sits when Baba gives darshan through her. His love and consciousness was palatable. I thought, *This is no side-show trans-medium platform. This is holy ground indeed.*

My only slight disappointment was no one had a copy of the book about the temple that I could buy to share with others. Having first seen pictures of the miracle manifestations from the website promoting the book, Shree Shirdi Sai Baba of South San Francisco, it was an initiation in itself to see them in person and be guided around to each. As if Baba heard my thought, I was immediately drawn to a radiant woman in the corner.

I shared a bit of my journey to the temple and she answered questions and shared precious stories of her own. Afterwards she handed me the first of many miracles I've witnessed there since, a carnation that was given to her, by Ashu, after bhajans concluded. When she held up the flower I watched vibhuti spring forth in a stream like I had personally experienced many years earlier, spontaneously manifesting from the fingertips of Sathya Sai Baba. Gwyn McGee further delighted me by pulling out a copy of the very book I sought. With an exhale in wonderment of the divine order of Baba's play, I discovered I had walked right over to the co-author of the book herself; the only one present with a copy of the book I had so wanted.

May I humbly offer without qualification, that from that day forward, every time I go to the mandir, visit Shree or her family, speak with a member of the community, write a prayer request, or simply call on Baba's name, I am intimately and uniquely blessed every time. If I but 'have eyes to see and ears to hear'... To give you a feel for the range and the realms of the miraculous, Baba lays like a feast before us. A few examples follow:

When we go up for darshan with Baba through Shree, we

are given a small white piece of paper to hold whatever Baba may choose to give us. Once Baba gave me the lei…garland from around his neck. I returned to my seat and noticed drops of what seemed like water dripping from some of the flowers. I was drawn to watch the drops on the paper in case, who knows, it might materialize into something. Indeed, it did.

The liquid was some kind of sweet nectar that formed into a few crystalline pieces of sugar the community calls "misri", tiny sugar cube manifestations. As soon as I thought I knew what it was, it changed. Some of the sugar drops morphed before my eyes, on the paper in my hand, into a tiny sugar statue of Baba.

A few days later while I facilitated a "Breakthru Consulting" session with a family who have long gone to Shree's, I shared the little miracle story. They said they wanted to see it. So, I took my personal Baba murti from my home altar along with the new little sugar statue I had laying on his lap, and asked Baba's grace to reside over our session. They loved seeing the manifestation and shared many of their own. But when we packed everything up to leave, I forgot to secure the tiny sugar statue and it somehow disappeared.

Later I prayed to Baba, kicking myself that I had lost that precious little power object. A few days later I noticed one little rectangle shaped piece of misri back on Baba's lap on my altar. I tried to pick it up to look at it. This time it was securely there. I can turn the murti upside down and the misri remains; as if Baba, knowing me, materialized and glued it there himself.

****

Navaratri, the victory of the Light over the Dark, was being celebrated, and on the last day of that nine day celebration of the various forms of the Goddess, I took the occasion to pray… do mantras to the Goddess Durga.

During my next darshan of Baba, without a word, He handed me a carnation and then pulled it back. I watched Him lift the flower in His right hand; scrunch it a few times until out popped a beautiful golden locket of Durga. It was surrounded by stones that looked like diamonds. This was auspicious not only because of the day, and the magnitude of the gift, but my secret sense of somehow needing Durga's various weapons/siddhis/powers in relation to the political and personal challenges I was engaged in at the time.

To my great sadness, a short time later, in my 'busy-ness' I ignored an intuitive warning, and the purse where I kept the locket was stolen from my car. This was an even louder wake up call to be more rigorously present and responsive in the moment and, yes, not attached, while forgiving myself and, this time, the thief. I mentioned it to Baba who, with a simple nod, said basically, "Swaha…things come and they go".

I thought, *Everything belongs to the Divine and it is Baba's leela. Who am I to say, how long it should stay? Did I really think an embodiment of Durga could be "mine"?*

Over the next couple of days I meditated on it, tried to integrate the lessons, and not make myself wrong, while blessing the young man I saw break into my car, affirming that Baba must have seen he needed the contents of my purse more than I did.

One night before I blew out my candle, in gratitude I put it all in Baba's hands. I awoke the next morning and the piece of fruit I had on my altar from the mandir had what first seemed like a big bruise or age spot on it. When I looked more closely, I saw it was a big heart. It was as if Baba was saying, "Did you forget to remember, Lynn, everything is love: Locket…

no locket... purse ... no purse ... license ... thief ... Baba ... Durga – all is Love. Don't get stuck in the form." Now, how yummy is that?

****

One day not long ago, while driving up to a stop light after leaving the gas station, I thought of a conversation I had with my sister the day before. She asked me, "Beyond healings, what do you think the practical point of miracle manifestations are? Whether it be a rudraksha bead coming out of a carnation or eye witnesses actually observing the long "deceased" Shirdi Sai Baba or Sathya Sai Baba actually walking around the temple in physical form? (embodying Shree)

I pondered out loud, "I'm sure Baba has a purpose for each. To me, they're like a heavenly kiss that opens a different channel to the divine. At once, they open the heart and mind in wonderment of unlimited possibility while creating an ever-so-personal immediate experience of grace." I remember liking the sound of that and, in gratitude, saying Baba's mantra "Om Sai Ram". As God is my witness, at that very moment, the car behind me honked to get my attention. A young Indian man got out and pointed at my car, "Hey, Lady, your gas cap is open." I laughed out loud as I thanked the man, screwed on the hanging cap and smiled. "Thank you, Baba!" God is real and all is taken care of even before we ask.

****

Being with such a Master can also shake you to your core. My friends, Miriam and Sheila, met Shree and Baba in South San Francisco soon after I did. They had been Shirdi Sai Baba devotees through another teacher for several years. When Sheila expressed her deep love to Baba at darshan, Baba said, "I know" and manifested a locket for her with His picture on it. As she walked back to her seat in the temple, she noticed one of the rhinestones encircling the photo was missing; and when she sat down she looked all over for it. Her mind raced. She wondered what He must think of her? What she must have done wrong that he would give her something "flawed".

Down stairs, in the living room, after eating the evening's prasad she told me the story. At that moment I happen to look down. Between her feet on the floor, there was a little stone that fit perfectly into her locket! Needless to say we all got our own lessons from that. As wonderful as it was they did not return to the mandir until over a year later.

Miriam suffered with cancer, and over the months it worsened. She lost so much weight she was gaunt and bedridden.

I asked Baba about her. He looked … and said compassionately, "She's not going to make it."

"I thought that as well," I said. "If there is nothing you can do, Baba, should I have she or Sheila come here anyway? Or is there anything else I can do to make it easier for her?"

Baba looked again and smiled. " I like her. I really like her. I will take care of her."

I thanked Him. Who could ask for anything more?

Miraculously, Miriam had an almost immediate turn around that shocked her family, doctors, and friends and filled them with wonderment. Her pain dissipated. She began to radiate such light and was up and running around re-connecting with family and friends, some, who never really knew her until then. "Sai Ram!"

I went through my own challenge with Baba, a year later when Miriam's condition suddenly took a nose-dive. Fully jaundiced and again at death's door, I updated Him on Miriam and another friend who had advanced cancer.

He said, "I am with her. I will heal them."

In the days that followed I didn't know whether to tell Sheila and Miriam or not. I could not tell if this was a test of my faith; whether Baba was actually going to resurrect Miriam again; or what He meant by "healing" when she was clearly dying. So, I held all possibilities like an unfolding mystery. I visited her on what surely seemed, and turned out to be, our last time together; where very important work was done wrapping up her life, including her requests for her transition ceremony and deep prayers of surrender to Jesus and Baba. An amazing photo was taken after I departed. A huge golden light above Miriam's bed appeared with a couple of subtle faces clearly visible in what looked like a golden portal to the next dimension.

The next day, still slightly agitated with how to hold Baba's promise, I texted Shree to update Baba that the end seemed near. When I pushed 'send', I let go of thinking somehow I was in control of any of this process, and a wonderful peace washed over me, emptying my mind and opening my heart. I knew Miriam was in Baba's hands and, somehow, all is well. A couple hours later, Sheila called to say that Miriam had passed at 6:15 pm. The exact moment my phone showed I was texting Baba … or was it the other way around?

But my lessons in all this were not yet fully integrated. The next time Baba came through Shree, I thanked Him for all He did for Miriam and for linking me with the exact time of her transition.

"I was with her," He said. "I told you I would heal her," as if mirroring back and inviting my deep question.

"Thank you so much, Baba. But why did you say you would

heal her? Why didn't you just tell me the truth that this was her time?"

"Lynn, she called me to take her; said she wanted to come home; that she was done. Had I healed her she would not have had a quality of life because too much damage had happened to her body."

"I understand and thank you with all my heart, Baba. But why didn't you just tell me that, like you did last year?"

"No one wants to know their friend is going to die."

"But, Baba," I argued. (Imagine, the privilege of this encounter...) "Satya (truth), Baba. I always want the truth from you. Please, Baba," I begged. "Satya must be our first agreement or how can I totally trust you? You dishonor me with a half truth if it is just temporary relief within an illusion."

We shared no more words out loud. He blessed me. I bowed and returned to my seat across the room. Through Shree's eyes, Baba glared deeply into me several times as I sat wrestling with my perceived crisis as the bhajans rang out.

As I sat there, He then took me into another dimension where I saw the limits of my thinking, the depth of my subtle doubt for any spiritual master in physical form, and, my not seeing that He could well have been telling me "the truth" at the time; yet Miriam's prayers to Him, which Sheila confirmed as almost exactly what Miriam said before she passed, and a myriad of other factors may have evolved that truth.

Later, so as not to burden Shree personally with my questions, I processed what was still not fully clear for me with my friend, Dhiren, over the phone. As I shared my embarrassment over challenging Baba at all after experiencing such a series of miracles; he understood I was still honestly wrestling with a deep question (as if I could possibly understand all that Baba knows and does and what realms Baba's healings happen in).

I soon realized that Baba had not actually told me last year when Miriam was going to pass; just that she "wasn't going to make it"; which she ultimately didn't. He just gave her, and me, a year longer of quality life. I confused his recent promise to "heal her" to possibly mean physical healing, because "taking care of her" included the year we were given.

This time, other dimensions of repair, for not only Miriam but those around her, were at work, that only he could see the implications of and the timing for. My challenge was not that he didn't physically heal her but that he didn't think I could handle the truth if he wasn't going to help her in the way he thought I preferred. Dhiren and I discussed my "trust" issue as ultimately a limit in my trust and perception of myself, which the clarity of the Master, in this case reflected.

I began to feel a whole other level of exquisite blessing from this year-long, multi-chapter experience with Baba through Shree. Beyond their divine ability to physically heal Miriam at will and understand when that is appropriate and when it is not; what touched me to my soul, was: His infinite compassion for my limited seeing; His loving willingness to receive my raw engagement with what He so generously shared; not to mention His supreme ability to consciously intercede with Miriam's soul upon her request, while simultaneously including me in the mystical union.

I also could not help but reflect what it is to be in Shree and her family's aura of love, with their angelic level of service and sacrifice. Throughout this year, I'd witnessed Shree fully take on the symptoms of many of those Baba is healing - to her own personal, temporary detriment, which can be at once heart wrenching, while spiritually liberating, for those around her.

She may be living out the pain of someone's cancer, coughing from pneumonia or fainting from anemia, but when Baba comes through and she is there as Him, together they demonstrate no such human limitation. It is quite a phenomenon to witness, and an amazing ongoing teaching to be with. Shree's surrender and the whole family's faith in Baba are beyond humbling, and mind-blowing to be around. It is the Great Mystery unfolding in unexplainable ways every day.

As my Sai Family friend, Dhiren, and I explored the contrast of my loss of Miriam with all that I'd gained through this divine process, all of a sudden, the mind was empty, the heart full and … ahhhh, once again, that sublime peace came forth that bathed every cell of my being.

I said, "Dhiren, can you feel it? THIS is exactly what I felt when Miriam transitioned. Can you feel it? Hmmmm. THIS is Baba's grace. And I'm sure THIS is what they mean by, 'the peace that passeth understanding'.

"Yes", my friend said. "This is what it's like at the mandir, if we just leave our minds outside".

"Hmmmm", we both sighed, as we settled into the Holy Presence.

"Om Sai Ram"

There are no words to express what it means to be around the one and only Shree Lal, who is clearly a saint in her own right, and our whole Sai family, with the great avatar Shirdi Sai Baba and all the multi-dimensional goings on at the mandir. All I know is that my heart can barely contain it and, gloriously, my mind will never fully grasp it. But this I am sure of: all who enter the doors of "our Little Shirdi" are supremely blessed. And I am eternally grateful.

JAGINDAR PRASHAD

This happened during a time when Shree was very sick. She was throwing up blood every day and that particular Thursday, during bhajans, Baba threw up some blood and they wiped Baba's mouth with a towel. Eventually Baba got up and started walking. Asish Chandra and Bakul Patel were on each side of Him. Baba walked toward Shree's room. I was a guru-mukh by then and I touched His feet as He passed by. Baba changed directions and I had an opportunity to touch His feet again. When I did, Baba stopped, looked down at me and placed His hand on my head. His hand had to be shaped like a claw because of how it fit on the top of my head. Baba turned my head slightly to the side and up, and I could see Him. He looked so large and He held me like that for maybe a couple of minutes. After that Baba did something I don't have the words to describe but ...He pulled my face forward a bit...and it was as if my whole face was no longer in the mandir! Baba's hand was still on my head but my face was on the other side... in another dimension. That's exactly what I thought when He held me like that. "I am on the other side now." I managed to tilt my head a bit more and I could really see Baba. Baba's face was no longer Shree's face when He comes through her.. It was different... and Baba appeared to be standing in thin air! I could see His robe...His feet...and He was standing in thin air! I was no longer in the mandir! It was an amazing experience. When I spoke to Don (Olds), who was sitting next to me when this happened, he said Baba had His hand on my head for more than three minutes. After that experience, for a while, my entire life's focus was on Baba and the mandir, and I looked at documentaries to gain more knowledge. I waited a few weeks before I told anyone about this. It was out of this world. Baba really gave me something that day.

****

I have looked in Baba's eyes and seen space...the cosmos. This happened. Once during darshan in South San Francisco, Baba asked me, "What yuga is this?"

I hesitated for a second, "This is Kali Yuga."

"This is the end of the Kali Yuga. Meri rakshanaya. This is all my doing," He said. "There is a twelve year process of cleansing. In 2024 the change will come."

Later when I thought about the Mahabharat and the part where Krishna and Arjun are in the chariot in the middle of the battlefield, Krishna said, "This is my rakshanaya."

It is no ordinary person in South San Francisco.

****

Baba normally comes into Shree by a certain time to give darshan. If He doesn't come by that time he usually doesn't come. This particular Thursday I knew there were people waiting, who really wanted to see Baba and the time had passed. I began to pray. I told Baba about the people and I asked Him to come. After a few minutes I felt this energy pass through me, and seconds later a flower fell from one of the murtis into Baba's water that always sits up front. I looked at Justin (Lal) and he saw the flower fall too. I looked at Shree and Baba had come into her at that precise time.

CHANDRA PRASHAD

Since I've been attending bhajans at the South San Francisco mandir I always have eye contact with the Shirdi Sai Baba murti that is in the front. One day, in 2013, I was seated in the back, as usual, and I looked in His eyes. All of a sudden my body got so warm and I started to cry. I began to speak to Baba from my heart about a lot of things and Baba's eyes began to move left to right. I thought, *Oh my God. Whatever I am thinking Baba is answering my prayer.* I thought of my daughters, particularly Patricia. I thought, *Patricia has been married for seven years and she has not been pregnant. I am kind of worried. Before something happens to me, Baba, make sure this comes true. That she becomes pregnant.*

After the puja I came home, and I did what I usually do before I go to bed. When I closed my eyes this time I said to Baba, *Please let my dream come true. Today or tomorrow. Anyday. I just want to know that this is going to happen.*

The next day Patricia was throwing up. I thought maybe she had the flu or something. Soon after that, my husband, Jagindar (Prashad) and I were sleeping in the mandir at my house and I thought about Patricia in my heart. I looked at Baba's murti, closed my eyes and something touched me on my shoulder right before I heard, "Wake up. Your dream has come true."

The next day I was out of town and I received a phone call from one of my daughters. She said, "Mom, do you know something? Patricia is pregnant."

Oh my God! Baba answered my prayer.

****

I had two brothers. My younger brother would go to his sisters' houses, get raksha bandhan tied, or we would go to his house because he was always prepared with a big dinner and everything to celebrate. After he died I never tied anywhere. I put my raksha bandhan next to my Krishna Bhagawan or Baba.

This particular raksha bandhan I was at the South San Francisco mandir. Everybody was there; all the brothers. Shree was tying raksha bandhan. I just sat there. I didn't want to show how I really felt to anyone, but inside I was just crying and crying.

I looked at Baba's murti and all of a sudden Shree got up from the chair where she had been tying raksha bandhans. She walked so fast into the other room and came back wearing Baba's clothes. Shree tied Baba's bandana on her head and went and sat in Baba's chair at the front of the mandir. The next thing I knew she called me.

"I'm your brother," He said. "Come tie raksha bandhan on me."

I cried. I sat on the floor and I held Baba's feet and I cried.

"Don't cry. I know what you were thinking," Baba said. "I read your heart."

I tied the raksha bandhan on Baba and He tried to give me some money.

"I don't want any money, Baba. I am so happy I have my brother here."

That day I experienced money flowing from Baba's hand. He was giving money to everybody. Baba was giving out hundreds.

I took the money but I didn't want to use it because Baba gave it to me for raksha bandhan. But one day we came across a hardship and I used that money because I had no choice. I said to Baba, "Please Baba forgive me for using your money."

****

Some of my family and I did nine Thursdays' Vrat and Puja. One of the days was Shivaratri. It was me, my son-in-law, Justin (Lal), Alicia and Sandy, my daughters. The last Thursday, among other things, we prepared food for the homeless and gave it out, and we made a mala for Baba.

We attended bhajans at the South San Francisco mandir when our puja was complete. After the bhajans we did aarti and we were given malas because it was our last Thursday of the Vrat. We went home from the mandir and took the malas straight to our mandir. As we were doing that, my husband and Sandy felt this whoosh of air go by. When we went into our mandir we saw two of Baba's murtis that we performed the Vrat and Puja with had vibhuti. Vibhuti did not come on the other two murtis. One of the murtis that it did not come on was mine.

Shree was in India the entire time. Later that day, after the vibhuti came on Baba's murtis, I spoke to Shree on the telephone. She told me everything was going good but she said during Shivaratri Justin brought a lobster home and I cooked it. Because of that the vibhuti only came on two murtis. It would have come on all four murtis. Shree told us that from Shirdi. We did not know we were doing something wrong.

Sindoors continue to come in our mandir, red kumkum, orange sindoor, and Baba's vibhuti.

****

In 2013 my husband, Jagindar, brought a single, white carnation home that Baba had given him during a Thursday darshan. After bhajans he came home and I placed the flower in our mandir. Over the next few days my husband did his prayers as usual, and on Tuesday he did the Hanuman Chalissa. I did my prayers too, but on Thursday while I was praying I looked at the flower and it was more open.

"What is this?" I said. I looked a little closer and a big rudraksh had come out of the center.

I went to my husband. "Dad, the white flower, did you see anything in there?"

"No. There was nothing," he said. "It was just a flower."

"There is something. If you want to look, come and look," I told him.

He saw the big rudraksh.

Later he asked Shree about it.

"How many lines are there?" she asked.

"There are five."

"Wear it," she replied. "It is very good for your health."

SHUSHEEL RAM

My thumb was bent for a long time. For more than six months I could not move it and the doctor wanted to operate. In February, 2013 I saw Shree at the San Bruno Temple.

"Make sure you come to Shirdi's place," she said. "Make sure you come on Thursday."

So, I went that following Thursday and sang bhajans. Baba never touched me. Nothing. But my heart was so full of Baba.

Bhajans were over and I was going down the stairs from the mandir when I hit my thumb against the stair railing. There was an instant pain that went straight into my thumb and it started moving again. My thumb is fine now.

REYNEL RUIZ A.K.A. GANESH

The first time I went to South San Francisco was in 2004. At that time Richard (Dick Selby) announced he was making a pilgrimage to San Francisco. He planned to take several people but one of them was not going and there was room for another person. So I decided to take the trip, which was scheduled the following week.

That night I had a dream where Shirdi Baba came and said, "I am inviting you for My birthday."

In the dream I replied, "Ohhh, your birthday."

That Thursday when we arrived at the temple Richard told us that there had been times when people traveled to the temple to see Baba but He didn't come, so Mr. Selby told us not to be disappointed if Baba didn't show up. I told Mr. Selby about my dream, and Mr. Selby said it was very interesting because he didn't think it was Baba's birthday. During the session we found out it was Baba's birthday. They brought in a cake and Baba wrote His age on it. I thought it was amazing to have such an experience, but I still had some doubts.

I returned to South San Francisco in 2011. It was after

Sathya Sai Baba passed away. Two friends, Sun Park and Sean Dee called me. They said they were going and asked if I wanted to come. I said I would. While we were there Baba came. I was amazed by it, and I had these spiritual feelings about Baba coming to her, but I wanted to know what was really happening. Does she really become Baba? And...I wanted to experience it again.

We went there two more times. Each time I had a spiritual experience, tears, etc., but eventually I came to the conclusion there was no way for me to really know what was happening. So I gave up.

In 2012 Gurupurnima was coming and I received a phone call from Sun.

"Ganesh, we are going. Would you like to come with us?"

"No-o, not this time." I had some issues about immigration on my mind.

Later I was at the Malibu Hindu Temple where I work, and I was praying to Baba about it. I told Him, "Baba I leave it in your hands. If it happens it happens. I leave it all up to you." Right after my prayer I got a phone call. It was Sean.

"Ganesh, you've got to come to our home. We've got a super surprise for you."

That was Sunday. I told him, "Monday I will not be able to go, but Tuesday for certain I will make it."

When I went into their house, that Tuesday, Sean said, "Sit here. And you have to hold a flower because when I start singing something very miraculous will start happening." I did as he said and he started singing.

"Jagadambe...Jagadambe...Jagadame."

As I sat there with my eyes closed it felt as if something was falling on my head. When I opened my eyes I saw Shree! And it was lots of vibhuti falling on me. Shree was visiting their house.

Right away She sat down. Baba came because of the singing.

"Are you surprised to see me?" Baba asked. "I know this time you didn't want to come to South San Francisco. So South San Francisco came to you." Then Baba told me. "You want to see your mom."

I said, "Ye-es."

"Don't worry. You will go in 2013. All your immigration problems will be solved."

How did He know about my immigration problems???

"The last time you were in South San Francisco Baba gave you a pendant. Where is the pendant?"

"I lost it in Mount Shasta," I replied. I was surprised because I knew I was being asked because He…She knew I had lost it.

"Don't worry," She said. "I will ask Him to give you another one."

The next day Shree came to my home, and visited my bhajan hall. I cooked food for them and showed Shree lots of photographs. She saw photos of Ma Bharosha, and asked, "Did she help you?"

"Yes," I told her. "She helped me a lot."

"Good," Shree replied.

Because it was officially Gurupurnima, we asked Shree if we could sing a couple of bhajans and do the aarti.

"Yes," she said. "But don't call Baba. If Baba comes and you are not prepared it is dangerous."

"Oh no we will not call Baba," I promised, but as soon as she sat in front of the altar she went into the mood. We wanted to stop it but we didn't know how. Sean sang a Ganesh bhajan, Sun, Pranam, and as soon as I began to sing a Krishna bhajan She was completely Baba. At that moment we were in shock. We didn't know what to do. We didn't have anything! Finally, we put a turban on His head and put a sari around Him.

He sat with His fist tucked under His ear and one leg tucked under Him with the other knee raised. He kept looking at His foot. We thought, *Why is He looking at His foot?* When I looked at His foot again...there was a beautiful, hibiscus flower between His big toe and the second toe. *Where did it come from?* I thought. We realized this yellow hibiscus had materialized.

"The reason I had to come here tonight," Baba said, "is to bless you. All your wishes will be fulfilled."

So during that visit I actually got the proof that Baba comes to her.

The next day we drove Shree back to South San Francisco. Usually I initiate singing bhajans but that day I was quiet. I was quiet because I felt like I was in Puttaparthi. Normally when Shree speaks her voice is so sweet. Her voice was not like that in the car, and there was this wonderful fragrance. We were all so very happy driving to South San Francisco.

When Baba came during the Gurupurnima celebration, and I went up for darshan, He said, "Thank you for the food and... It was never Shree. It was Me all the time."

That was my answer as to why I felt I was in Puttaparthi.

ANANTH SAMAI

My spiritual experiences started out with Amma...Amirtanandamayi. She travels around hugging people. I became friends with a few devotees at her ashram and one day in 2007 someone invited me to come and experience Sai Baba at Shree's house. I couldn't believe what I heard; that Shirdi Sai Baba manifested through a Fijian lady. I was very curious and I wanted to see for myself.

I went with some friends from the ashram, and the very first day that I went it really got my attention. Baba came and He literally walked around the mandir and basically got close to everyone, which is a little different from what He does now-a-days. Now He sits in a chair and people go up and see Him. At that time He walked around.

When He came to me I noticed His eyes were really sharp and piercing. That look really got my attention. I immediately felt that there was some kind of connection between us and I was curious. Even though I had heard about Him I wanted to know more. I felt drawn to Baba for some reason.

I started going to the South San Francisco mandir. My

friends were not interested at that time. They felt if they went once a year or once every six months that was good enough. But I felt the need to go back more often.

I started going regularly and I started to go by myself.

While I was going there was a battle in my mind. The battle was...'I am worshipping two gurus'.

I'd heard from many swamis in the past that you should not have two gurus. You should only have one. The reason being, if this guru says X and the other guru says Y and the two things are opposing things...two different things, what do you do? It can be confusing for the spiritual seeker. So I had a big battle going on in my mind because I was devoted to my guru, Amiritanandamayi, but at the same time I felt drawn to Shirdi Sai. I couldn't give up either. I didn't want to give up either.

Eventually I asked one of Amma's swamis. I told him I was drawn to Shirdi Sai but I considered Amma as my guru. What to do?

He advised me when I worshipped Amma to visualize her with a beard and wearing Sai Baba's attire. I attempted it but it didn't solve my problem.

One Thursday I went to the South San Franscco mandir and Baba came and gave darshan as usual. I went up to see Him and He did something very strange. He hugged me.

"I Am your Divine Mother," He said.

That hug was no ordinary hug. It felt exactly the same as when Amma hugs. Amma has a very unique way of holding the person. A very gentle way. When Baba hugged me it felt the exact same way as when Amma hugs me.

Amritanandamayi is worshipped as the Divine Mother, but Baba knew what was going on in my mind. At first I didn't think much about it but afterwards I felt wow...He really understood the constant battle that was inside of me.

A few weeks later I went up and received darshan from Him again.

"Did you notice what I'm wearing?" He asked.

I looked at Him. "No, Baba."

"You haven't noticed what I'm wearing? I am wearing white just like your Amma."

I gathered that He was reiterating that He and Amma were not separate. They are one in the same. That brought a lot of peace to my mind as to whom do I go to. It made me realize it doesn't matter. It also made me realize that Baba could really read people's minds.

****

There was a time when I was sitting in the mandir and Baba was giving darshan to everybody else. I was going through something and I prayed to Him silently as He gave darshan. I looked up and He was staring right at me, and then Baba shook His head motioning 'Yes'. He heard the plea of my prayer and He indicated He knew I was praying to Him by shaking His head.

****

Several years ago I convinced a group of my friends, who are Amma devotees, to come with me to the South San Francisco mandir. This resulted in a larger, than usual, number of Amma devotees in attendance. One of the devotees sang a bhajan and a strange thing occurred; a hugging frenzy started at the mandir. Baba began to hug everybody during darshan. Although I had gotten several of my friends to come I really wasn't in a social mood, so I sat in the back and watched what was happening. I decided not to go up for darshan and I really didn't think anyone would notice in that crowd.

Darshan was over and it was time for aarti. All of a sudden Shree's husband, Dhiren, came and found me in the back.

"Baba said you did not give Him a hug."

I was so surprised that I was singled out, and that Baba called me for a hug. I went up and hugged Baba, but this hug was definitely different from the first hug when Baba said, "I Am your Divine Mother". This hug was more of a strong manly hug. It was not Amma's unique, gentle hug.

Of course my mood changed for the better after that, and I realized when you need Him Baba is always there for you.

SRINIVASULU & SUBHASHINI SANIGEPALLI

In 2008 I lived in an apartment in Fremont, California. At that time the Lal family owned and operated an Indian store in the same city. During a visit to our home in January or February, Shree stood with my wife, Subhashini, and me in front of our apartment building. She said, 'I will come and sleep at your house. I don't know why but it will happen.'

A couple of months later, while Baba was giving darshan in the South San Francisco mandir, He told us the same thing; one day He would sleep in our home. Months passed. In August we travelled to India but before we left, during another darshan we asked Baba to come and sleep at our home.

"There is a lot of time," He said. "Don't worry. You go and come back."

So we went to India and returned.

After the trip activities around our quest to buy a new home increased. An exciting opportunity arose and we decided to discuss the matter with Baba. I could hardly wait for the next darshan.

"What do you want me to do?" I asked Him when the time arrived.

"I will tell you later," was His only reply.

I wish He had said more but that was all He told us.

Days later we received a much awaited communication for an appointment, and a deadline for entries was scheduled the following week. Uncertain, we sought Baba's advice.

"Should we take it, Baba?" we asked during the next bhajan.

"Take it. Purchase the home," He said. "I need a house to live in."

He gave that advice in November or December of 2008.

By March, 2009 our house was under construction. Once the house was built Subhashini and I decided to have a house warming. We knew Shree was taking classes in Fremont and we hoped she would agree to attend our ceremony. We were not disappointed. A date was set. Filled with anticipation we extended a formal invitation to everyone, including Shree, the following Thursday.

A day or so later I received a telephone call.

"Should I bring Baba's clothing to your house warming ceremony?" Shree asked.

I was so surprised I was totally speechless. "Of course! Yes Please!" I finally managed to say.

Our housewarming day arrived. A respectable number of devotees and family members attended the ceremony, which included bhajans. As Shree anticipated Baba came during the devotional singing. Although Shree indicated Baba might come, the truth is I could not imagine Baba coming in my house, so when He came I was not prepared.

Suddenly I found myself looking for a chair for Baba. As we had not fully moved into our new home we did not have a house full of furniture. So what did I do? I got a small chair and covered it as well as I could.

Baba looked at the chair. "I can't sit in that. The chair will break."

You see, Baba is very, very heavy when He comes through Shree.

"I didn't expect you, Baba," was all I could say.

Baba made everything easy. He sat on the floor in a special space we prepared for Him and He gave Subhashini and me darshan.

"Are you happy?' He asked.

"We are very happy, Baba," we replied and He allowed us to wash His feet.

Next to our pleasure and surprise He manifested a Shivalinga.

"Do abhishekam with this Shivalinga," He instructed, "And do puja with it."

Then Baba said, "I have given you darshan. Now I am going."

"No, Baba. Don't go," I pleaded. "There are people who have come from different places. Please give them darshan too."

Baba smiled. "I knew you would say that," He replied, and Baba gave personal darshan to everyone in attendance.

After everyone received darshan I told Baba I needed a more stable job.

"Don't worry. A job is getting ready for you."

I was happy to hear those words.

"My daughter has class tomorrow morning," He continued. "She will sleep here tonight. Do you need anything else before I leave? Or should I ask my daughter to leave tonight?"

"No, no, no," I replied, surprised by the turn in events.

"So you are asking me and I am staying," were His final words.

We had a little food after that and one by one our guests left. That night Subhashini and Shree slept on the floor with a comforter and a heater. Shree asked me not to worry about where she slept.

"I can sleep on the floor," she assured us. "I will be fine."

Later Subhashini told me, in the early morning hours perhaps 5 a.m. or so, she was twisting and turning because she was uncomfortable. She said she mumbled, "Sai Ram. Sai Ram," softly as she turned, and to her surprise she heard Shree reply, "Sai Ram." Subhashini said she thought, *Why is she awake this time in the morning?* So she looked at Shree and she got the surprise of her life. Her face was no longer Shree's but the face of Baba when He comes. Not only that, Baba was giving her a blessing with both His hands. About a month later I got a more stable job. I have that same job to this day.

****

My wife and I are gurumukhs, chosen by Baba, and Subhashini likes to perform washing of Baba's feet. One day during the summer of 2011, after visiting another devotee's home, Shree came to my home and Baba came.

"What do you want to do?" He asked.

"I want to wash your feet, Baba."

"If you want to do...go ahead and do. Ask all the gurumukhs in this house to do it. Tell them they are to repeat the gurumukh mantra in their mind as they wash My feet. I began to wash Baba's feet along with the other gurumukhs, but I was not repeating the mantra in my mind.

Immediately Baba said, "You are not saying the mantra. You are not doing it. Do it!"

He knew what was going on in my mind.

I was a contractor and that contract was ending soon. I went to see Shree at the Freemont grocery store. It was May, 2007. I was a little distracted because of my job situation.

"Why are you so sad?" Shree asked.

"My contract will end soon. I will get another but I will be missing payments for awhile."

She said, "Don't worry. Next time Baba comes talk to Him."

Easwaramma Day was the next occasion when Baba gave darshan and we attended the celebration.

"I will take care of you," He assured me.

I found the courage to ask, "How Baba?"

"I will take care of your job. Make sure you are here every Thursday."

One week later I got sick and because I was so sick I decided not to go to bhajans. I was asleep with my phone next to me when I got a phone call.

"Today I will pick you up and we are going to temple," a friend said as I listened.

"I can't go. I am sick. Throwing up and everything," I told him. "I have no energy. I am very sick."

He said, "No. I am coming to pick you up."

I had maybe fifteen minutes to get ready. I almost collapsed I was so weak. He picked me up and on the way to temple I threw up in the car. When I arrived I had a cup of water and went into bhajans. Immediately I was re-energized and had no symptoms, no feelings of the sickness. It was over! Baba's words are true.

My parents were visiting from India. The first week my mother was okay but during the second week she developed a lot of pain and couldn't breathe. She was taken to the emergency room and the doctors diagnosed that she had suffered a major stroke. My mom had that stroke on Mother's Day 2013. They also found a blockage in her heart and said she needed to have an operation where a stent could be inserted. The surgery was performed and the stent was put in place. My mother remained in the hospital for a week because she developed an infection. After we took her home we cared for her using the medications we had been given from the hospital. For three or four days we looked after her but then her condition changed; she developed a serious case of nausea and could not eat. We took her to the doctor and he recommended we take her back to the emergency room. She was on the table in the emergency room and my mother went into cardiac arrest. She had a heart attack! For five minutes they performed CPR and finally they were able to get my mother's heart to beat again. It took six hours to stabilize my mother but even then the doctors told us she was in critical condition and would be in critical condition for forty-eight hours. Because my mother was in cardiac arrest for so long the doctors were very concerned about what effect the heart attack may have had on her other organs. They feared some of her organs might have been damaged and decided to perform more tests.

It was at that time that I contacted Shree and told her what was happening to my mom. Shree asked many questions about my mother's condition. She wanted to know everything that happened. Once we contacted Shree the entire Sai family began to pray for my mom. While all of that was going on the doctors did not have much hope for my mother. They said she had a twenty percent chance of making it. When I told Shree she said, "Don't worry your mom will be fine."

Not long after that we received a phone call from Shree's home. It was her family. They told us Shree became very sick, and that she was constantly talking about my mom, thinking of her. I was totally surprised when I received a photograph of Shree from Sanjeev (Mason). He took the photograph of Shree as she lie sick in the bed because Shree had actually begun to look like my mom! From her nose to below her throat looked exactly the way my mother's body looked as she lie in the hospital bed! Shortly after I received that photo my mom's oxygen levels began to rise and slowly they removed all of the support systems from her. We were very relieved when my mother was eventually able to feed herself.

I went to the next bhajans and had Baba's darshan. Basically, He said, in Hindi, What's up? What is happening?"

"Thank you very much, Baba," I replied. "What did I do that You would help me like this?"

"I did nothing for you," Baba said. "Your sister took the pain."

"What did I do for her?" I asked Baba. "What was my relationship with her that she would help me like this?"

"You were related and had other lifetimes together. That is why she pours so much love on you. That's why she took the pain. Your mother will go through the medical procedures and that's okay. But you have faith in Me, and she will be fine."

Now, my mom is doing good.

RICHARD K. SELBY A.K.A. DICK

Beginning in 2001 and continuing to the present time (2012), I have been going on a regular basis to South San Francisco and the Shirdi Sai Temple. During this time, I frequently have brought with me other devotees from the Los Angeles area. The last trip was on September 29th, 2012 and approximately twenty of us made it to this most special Shirdi Sai Baba birthday celebration. We traveled in four different vehicles.

Throughout these past years, I have witnessed a variety of miracles: Baba producing various pendants from flowers, flowers from which vibhuti flowed, and flowers that have produced vibhuti over an extended period of time.

Two years ago in 2010, I was rained upon, as were others, with a special celestial candy that fell out of nowhere when the incorporation of Shirdi Sai Baba occurred. In this last trip one of the individuals who came received kumkum in her hair. This person also received a pendant. I, too, received a Shirdi Baba pendant. Others within this group received a variety of pendants and blessings, with no one going away empty handed.

I think, however, my most powerful experience dates back to Shirdi Baba's birthday in 2010. I had taken others with me, and driving to South San Francisco and back we had the most interesting conversations. One of the ladies, Sonia Francisca Cortez, was quiet during the outgoing trip and stated that she didn't feel well. On the way home Sonia told us that Baba had put His hands on her stomach. He then produced vibhuti from a flower and placed them in a piece of paper.

"When you get home, throw this in the ocean," He told her.

When Sonia arrived home she did as Baba instructed. Time passed before I heard about Sonia again, but what I heard was this: her cancer disappeared.

When I spoke to her on October 27, 2012 to confirm the account that I shared here and to get permission to use her name, Sonia validated the experience and assured me

"Fantastica!"

Baba had essentially taken Sonia's illness and its cause and transferred all those inherent bad qualities to the flower, which He instructed her to throw into the ocean. This is a similar method of alleviating illnesses or disease that Baba used when He lived as Sai Baba of Shirdi.

There is one last observation and I realize this relates directly to my enthusiasm about attending this Shirdi Baba Temple. The love that emanates from all of these individuals who live in this house and who assist is palpable. Shree's mother (Parvati) is always there for whomever might need assistance. The temple could not function without her. Shree also has four daughters (Manav, Inder, Kushbo, Shruti) and two sons (Justin and Shivam). All of these individuals, from the oldest to the youngest serve to make this Shirdi Baba Temple a loving, kind, compassionate environment where everyone feels welcome. Each in his or her own way reaches out to those who attend and Shree, after the incorporation occurs and everyone goes downstairs, continues this process of compassion and love. She frequently comes downstairs from the bhajan area and sits with everyone. It is Shree's presence, both as herself and when Baba is incorporated, that is the loving glue that fills the hearts of everyone who attends.

This Shirdi Baba Temple in South San Francisco is the magnet that brings people from all over the world and many thousands have attended. This Shirdi Sai Temple, Shree, and the entire family, serve all of us as we are blessed with love, kindness, miracles and Shirdi Sai Baba.

AVINASH AND SANDY SINGH

Avinash

In 2011 I had an experience that was very real but very different. I knew I was not dreaming. I knew I was not here on earth.

This happened early in the morning. I was lying down and when I woke up I woke up in a place where there was this bright light coming toward me. Out of that light stepped Baba, Shivaji and another person, but I couldn't see that person's face because it was very blurry. At that point I didn't know what was going on and Baba spoke to me.

"Let's go. It's your time to go."

I was quiet for a second. Baba was smiling and I looked at Shivaji and He had a smile on His face. They both looked at me and told me to go with Them. I had some health issues and I knew what time it was and I thought, *Oh my God! I am never going to see my family again!*

At that point I just dropped to the ground crying. I was scared. I couldn't look Them in the eyes. I begged for my life. I told them, "I can not go right now. Not now! I have kids. What about their future? I have a wife. Everything I am working on is not complete. There are a lot of things I need to do."

I knew They were going to take me somewhere that was good, that it was my chance to go with Baba, but still I begged, "Please! Please, Shivaji! Don't take me right now!"

I cried and cried after I spoke and I would not look up at Them. I knew it was not a dream and it wasn't any place on earth. I don't know where They took me or my soul. I can't describe it.

Then all I remember was I was back in my bed and my wife, Sandy, said I screamed for water. I don't remember doing that but she said that is what I did. Panicked she ran and brought me water. Immediately, I called Shree. I told her what had happened and I began to cry again.

"It was your last day on earth," she told me. "Baba gave you another life. The third person is the one who takes you away when you are ready to go," she said.

I knew I could only talk to Shree about this because everybody else would say it was a dream. I absolutely knew it was not a dream.

Baba gave darshan that next Thursday during bhajans. He called me to Him and explained what happened. Baba told me it was not a dream and that He had given me another life. He also told me I would have my third child. During that time my grandmother was sick and I asked about her.

"Baba is my grandmother going to make it or will she pass?"

"No, she will not make it. But in your time of sorrow I will give you happiness. I could have taken you with me but I have given you a new life." He also told me, "I am going to take something from you but in return I am going to give you something."

A few days later Sandy and I found out we were going to have another child.

Time passed and my grandmother died, but a week later my baby was born. Those important events happened right together. Something was taken and something was given.

I have been trying to take care of my health since I had that experience. I treasure this new life Baba has given me, and this new opportunity.

****

Sandy

One of the biggest experiences I've had and one that I really never forget happened in 2011 when I read the first book, Shree Shirdi Sai Baba of South San Francisco: Divine Touch.

I finished reading the last chapter of that book and I hurried down the stairs in my home to tell my family about it. I reached the bottom and the phone rang. My dad (Jagindar Prashad) answered it.

"Hello."

He listened and said, "Un-huh. Un-huh," to whoever was on the phone, and this puzzled look came over his face. Then he looked at me and asked, "Did you just finish reading a book?"

"Yes," I replied. "I just finished reading the book about Baba that Gwyn and Anita wrote."

"Well, you have a phone call."

"Who is it?" I asked.

"It's Baba."

"Oh my God! Are you serious???"

"Yes! He said you just finished reading a book."

This happened just as I had rushed down the stairs to tell

my parents that I had finished reading the book and that I felt Baba's presence in the room. The room smelled like vibhuti. It was all around me. Every time I picked up that book to read it I would smell vibhuti, but this time it was very strong. I also felt this draft of air and then I smelled jasmin flowers. So I was rushing down the stairs to tell them, "Guess what? I just finished reading the book and Baba was in the room with me! I know He was because I smelled His presence." But those words were stolen because before I could say anything my dad said, 'Baba is on the phone and He said you finished the book.'

****

There have been times when I didn't feel well that Baba has come and comforted me. I felt the bed go down from the weight of someone's body as if someone sat down. In February and March of 2012 I even felt Baba's heavy hands on my shoulders after He made me a gurumukh in the South San Francisco mandir.

I was sick for about two weeks and I started to chant the mantra I was given as a gurumukh. Baba came that night and put His hands on my shoulders, and the next morning I woke up and there was nothing wrong with me. No fever. Nothing. I thought, *Oh my God! Where did all my sickness go?*

****

My son began to struggle with his lessons in school. That had never happened before and we were concerned that perhaps he had a learning disability. Something seemed to be blocking him from doing the best he could in school.

I prayed to Baba about it. I promised to pray more, to spend more tiime in our puja room, to even pray at work. I also performed the Vras Puja. Once I completed that puja his performance in school was amazing. It still is.

During darshan Baba told me, "Always chant my name. Close your eyes and imagine my feet and you getting my blessings and everything will fall into place."

My life is going well. I got a really good job and I'm happy. Now I have three sons. Before Baba I was happy but I wasn't this happy. There was always stress of some kind, and even now there is the stress of everyday life but it is much less, and I am very happy and grateful.

"He had such patience with me, and Baba shared that vibhuti with everyone."

BAHADAR SINGH

On Sathya Sai Baba's birthday 2012, Baba made me a gurmukh. He gave me a mantra in my ear. With the music and all I received some of it...but not all of it.

My wife, Rita (Kaur), and I returned to Shree's home at a later date because I wanted Baba to give me the mantra again. We were all going to have lunch together, but before lunch Shree said she and I should go up into the mandir alone so Baba could give me the mantra in private. We were in the mandir only a few minutes when Baba came. I sat perhaps one foot in front of Him. He asked me the same questions He asked when He initially gave the mantra to me. When Baba told me the mantra again; He told me to write it. But I've been in the United States for so many years that I've forgotten how to write in my own language! Baba was patient with me. He told me the mantra three or four times and I was finally able to write it so I could remember it.

"You want anything more?" Baba asked.

I said, "Baba, everything is fine."

Next Baba said, "Can you stand me up so I can sit on the chair?" Baba was sitting on the floor.

"Yes," I replied, and I tried to lift Baba up but I could not.

Baba told me to call Inder or someone else from downstairs to help me.

Inder, Sanjeev, and my wife came to help but it was very hard to lift Baba up.

Finally we were able to put Baba in the chair and vibhuti came on Baba's head. There was no vibhuti when we came upstairs. Now there was lots of vibhuti in the middle of Baba's head. It was my understanding that normally Baba would give the mantra only one time. He had such patience with me, and Baba shared that vibhuti with everyone.

****

Three or four months before Shivam was born in 2010, a group of us were sitting downstairs after bhajans. First a few of us came downstairs, and a short time later Shree came down. It was perhaps 9:30 p.m.

My son was waiting to use the bathroom, and when Shree came down she also wanted to use the bathroom. I told my son to allow Shree to go in first but she objected and my son went in. When Shree finally went in the bathroom, from the size of her stomach, it was obvious she was expecting a baby.

Later when Shree sat on the couch she asked, "Anybody got any questions?"

We knew Baba normally asked that question but Shree's face did not look like Baba. Everybody thought it was Shree and not Baba.

Then "Shree" asked my wife and me, "Why don't you let him buy the puppy?"

We were surprised because we hadn't told anyone about a puppy; that our son wanted a puppy.

More time passed and my wife said, "Didi, we're going to have to go. We need to leave because of the drive back to Sacramento."

The reply, "I am not your Didi. Look. I don't have a baby in my stomach."

With my own eyes I saw there was no stomach. Shree would have been six or seven months pregnant at the time.

****

One Thursday bhajan, near the time of Raksha Bandan 2013, my wife told Shree that I wasn't feeling well. Shree looked in my hand, hugged me, and started crying.

During Raksha Bandan 2013 Shree Baba told me I was totally gone. He said I had died but that I was given a new life. I was told to be calmer and I am doing just that.

SHEKHAR SURABHI

The first time I met "Didi Shree" I was at Srinivas Sange-palli's house about four years ago... 2009. He had been telling me about this mandir in South San Francisco but some-how we didn't connect.

My wife, Madhavi, and I met Shree, her mom, and several other family members that day. Madhavi was expecting our first child. Suddenly, when Baba came it was a shock for me because it was my first time experiencing something like that. I remained in a kind of shock, even after Baba left her body. People were sitting around talking when Didi asked me to move her foot one inch. I tried but I was not able to move her foot. It was so hard. You can move an object about an inch... all you have to do is pull it, but this was very hard for me to do.

Four people tried to move her foot one inch. I got goose-bumps. I didn't know what to do. I never came up against any-thing like that in my life. What is she? Perhaps a hundred thirty pounds and I was a hundred forty-five pounds.

I could not move her single leg one inch. We tried a couple more times after her energy began to slow down and we were able to move it slightly.

While Baba was there He asked us to come to the Shirdi Temple in South San Francisco. Srinivas said it was unusual for Baba to ask people to come to the temple. Usually they asked Baba if they could come to the temple. He told us we were very fortunate that Baba had asked us to come. So the next Thursday we went to the mandir for the first time.

****

We became close to Shree's family and we asked her to come to our home. She agreed to come and then time passed and we waited and waited for her to come to our house.

Meanwhile I prayed to Baba. I asked Him to come to my house with vibhuti. I know that was a selfish kind of thing, praying to Baba for vibhuti, but that's what I did.

Suddenly, one day, Didi accepted my invitation. When she walked through my door in her hand was an idol of Shirdi Sai Baba with vibhuti on it.

I was told earlier that morning she was praying in the mandir and vibhuti came on that small Shirdi Sai Baba idol.

So when she came to my house Didi got out of the car and walked to my door with the idol in her hand. She said, "This is for you". I was stunned.

****

We were discussing families and children at the mandir. Didi told us we should go on and plan to have another child. She said if we waited it would be too late for my wife, Madhavi, to conceive. We had a three-year-old son, Nandan, at the time and she said that we should plan now. We thought that we would wait for a couple of years but she told us that would be too late. A couple of months after my wife conceived Baba told us that we would have a beautiful girl. We didn't do any of the scans or anything to find out if it was a girl. Now our beautiful daughter is one year old. Baba named her Saisha. Baba says Nandan has a special connection with Didi. He always sings Baba's bhajans.

The Mandir

AFTERWORD BY GWYN MCGEE

Initially, I thought there would be so many devotees clamoring to participate in this project that there would be room for only one experience per devotee. There is an abundant, complex history of devotees who have witnessed the evolution of Shree Sai Baba over the past decade. I, personally, have been privy to powerful devotee experiences that are not a part of this book. I can't imagine the number of devotee's lives that have been affected by what is occurring in South San Francisco. But one thing I know for certain: Nothing happens without His Sankalpa…His Will.

I say "Thank you" to the devotees who are published here; the number of experiences acquired through recorded interviews, and the four written/edited submissions are exactly what He intended. I must also take this opportunity to sincerely ask forgiveness for any small discrepancies devotees may find in their accounts. It was not intentional, and is simply due to my limitations; linguistic and otherwise. Know throughout this process I prayed to Baba, asking for what I needed for Him to be happy with all of us.

There is a special significance to the words, Devotees Speak, in the title. I attempted to maintain elements of the devotee's conversational style, in order that the reader might feel, while reading, engaged in an actual conversation with the devotee.

I believe Shree Sai Baba of South San Francisco: Devotees Speak was necessary to present an expanded view of the spiritual and physical reality that surrounds Shree Sai Baba.

Scholars have studied "possession" for centuries. Fear has accompanied this subject because of a widely spread acceptance of the concept of a wayward spirit inhabiting an unwilling human body, as opposed to a welcomed deity. From my limited research into a bottomless arena; there are two kinds of possession. Spirit possession. Deity possession. I've concluded, an aspect of what we are allowed to believe we experience in South San Francisco, the times when "Baba comes", is deity possession. Shree becomes and Avesha Avatara. I use the terms "aspect" and "allowed to believe we experience" because even deity possession does not explain, in totality, what occurs with Shree Sai Baba.

Bhakti induced Avesha Avatara is an accepted term associated with oracular deity possession...when, because of the love of His/Her devotees, the God or Goddess speaks, gives advice.

Those who have experienced South San Francisco know for certain the love is there and so is the Deity.

In closing, I will not in these few lines attempt to sum up South San Francisco's divine play. Like many, from time to time I too have a human need to make human sense of a Divine play; a need to examine the required human drama that ensures such divinity remains on this physical plane. But after compiling this book I ask myself, Why? Why-y, when overall lives are being saved and/or experiencing less suffering...when our oneness with divinity is being revealed...when moments of joy and gratitude are being experienced beyond conception. "Why question the divine drama that is Shree Sai Baba when nothing but LOVE would make a Being do the things that are shared here, in Devotees Speak."

JAI SAI BABA!